François Méchain
Brioude

François Méchain
Chambre d'écoute

2

Nils-Udo
Clemson Clay-Nest

3

Nils-Udo
Root Sculpture

4

Nils-Udo
Manglas

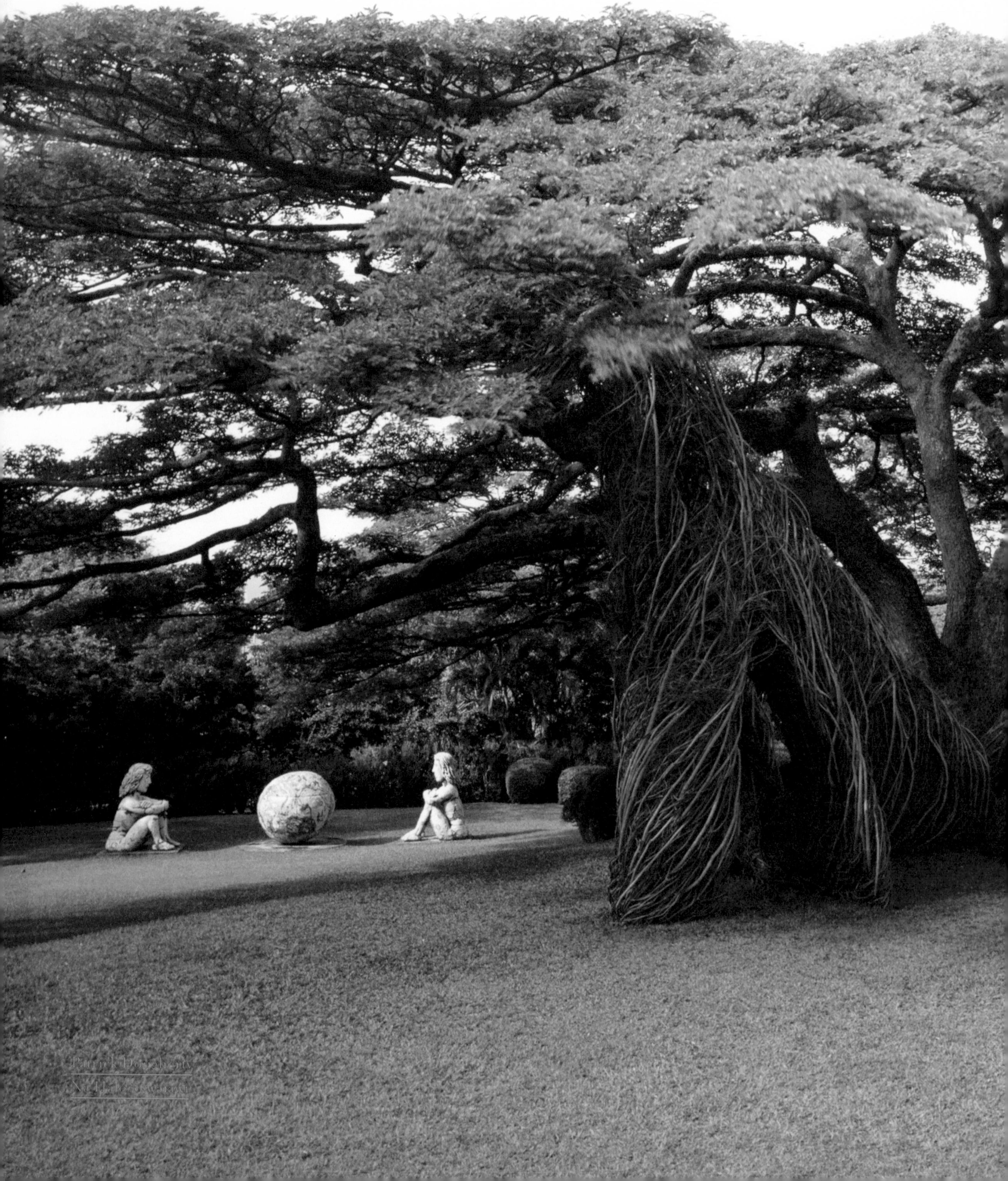

David Nash
Ash Dome

Architecture of Change

Sustainability and Humanity in the Built Environment

Kristin Feireiss, Lukas Feireiss (Eds.)

Contents

AESTHETICS OF PERFORMANCE

Preface
Kristin Feireiss

Kristin Feireiss is founder of the Aedes
Architecture Forum, Berlin together with
Hans-Jürgen Commerell and curator
of the Zumtobel Group Award.

Certainty about the finite nature of resources and the
insight that innovative solutions in architecture and town
planning in particular can contribute to the urgently needed
minimal use of energy and resources, and thus to improving
the quality of life, has increasingly been anchored in the public consciousness. The fact that the subject of sustainability is
not just high on the global political agenda now, but that artists and media stars are attaching themselves to this movement
and drawing attention to the dangers of global warming and
the associated consequences in campaigns, films and concerts
all over the world, has given a special thrust to this development. There has never been such a great consensus between
the public and politics as over the subject of climate change
and the question of how we can contribute innovatively and
constructively to improving our environment.

Questions about the responsibility of individuals and
the architecture profession are being raised again today. If the
connection between ethics and design has traditionally been
reduced to individual responsibility, with little or no attention paid to circumstances, to the specific situation in which
architecture works as design, now — as a result of the global
ecological crisis - people have started to address new responsibilities for architecture. Ethics, which was once restricted to
interpersonal relationships, now has to be extended to people's surroundings. Lines linking design to themes involving
environmental politics, lines linking design to questions of
sustainability, can be made out all over the world, and so can
new codes of behaviour. The artist Moholy Nagy, one of the
most important teachers at the Dessau Bauhaus in the early
20th century, formulated it like this: "Design is not a profession, it is an attitude to the world we live in."

These questions are not merely discussed by architects
and town planners all over the world, but increasingly realised
in their projects. Even so: globally speaking, sustainable
architectural concepts are still the exception rather than the

rule. Reason enough for businesses who are conscious of their
responsibility to stimulate and support environmental design
that treats resources with care so that they contribute to improving the environment with their commitment.

This book would never have come into being without
the Zumtobel Group, which is globally active with its headquarters in Dornbirn, Austria. In late 2006, Zumtobel
Group commissioned the Aedes Architecture Forum to develop an architecture prize for sustainability. When choosing
projects, a particular eye was kept on environment-friendli-
ness in interplay with the aesthetics of architectural language,
and on the humanitarian, ethical, social and economic added
value of the work.

The key to the award concept was a two-category structure — "Built Environment" and "Research and Initiative"
— with the intention of stimulating and promoting both
a pioneering realised building as well as research projects
and initiatives in this field. The jury members were Anna
Kajumulo Tibaijuka, Under Secretary of the United Nations
and Executive Director of the United Nations Human
Settlements Programme (UN-HABITAT), Nairobi; Peter
Sloterdijk, Professor of Philosophy and President of the State
Academy of Design in Karlsruhe; Peter Head , Director in
Planning and Sustainability at Arup, London; the archi-
tects Kazuyo Sejima, Tokyo; Stefan Behnisch, Stuttgart / Los
Angeles, Yung Ho Chang, Boston / Beijing, Colin Fournier,
London, Enrique Norten, Mexico City / New York and the
Chairman of the Executive Board and Chief Executive Officer
of the Zumtobel Group, Andreas Ludwig, Dornbirn.

Overall, the international and interdisciplinary jury
selected — from twenty projects in each category — one laureate
and four nominees. Around forty projects were submitted for
the "Zumtobel Group Award for Sustainability und Humanity
in the Built Environment," awarded in 2007 for the first

time. These projects provide the subject matter for this book, and were suggested to the jury by a team of international experts, including Jacopo Crivelli Visconti from Brazil, Erwin Viray from Singapore, Leon van Schaik from Australia and Nikolas Kuhnert from Germany.

The incredible breadth of the work presented, responding to different conditions and needs in the world's individual regions, embraces both the winning project for the Zumtobal Group Awards in the "Built Environment" category, the San Francisco Federal building by the American architecture practice Morphosis, and the victor in the "Research and Initiative" category, the Solar Updraft Tower by the German engineering practice Schlaich Bergermann Solar, which has so far been realised only in a model experiment.

To make the subject matter as a whole more accessible, the present publication has been structured into three key themes: Efficiency in the Everyday, Aesthetics of Performance and Didactics of Engagement. The works presented are embedded in different essays and interviews.

My thanks go to everyone who has contributed to this publication, the architects, the authors who have their say in essays and interviews, the Zumtobel Group and the Raiffeisen Zentralbank Österreich AG who made this publication possible through their generous support, and to Herbert Resch of Zumtobel, who collaborated with us to develop the idea for this initiative.

Foreword
Andreas J. Ludwig

Andreas Ludwig is Chairman of the
Management Board and Chief Executive
Officer of Zumtobel Group.

For many years now, taking responsibility for the environment and society has been a central element of our company's vision and values. Our core business is providing integrated lighting solutions for the professional lighting sector with a portfolio including innovative LED light sources, luminaires and control gear. This work carries with it a particular responsibility for the use of resources: just under 20 per cent of world electrical energy is used for artificial lighting alone, generating 1,900 million tons of CO_2 per year.

We have identified major energy-saving potential here. One essential tool in this context is replacing inefficient lighting systems, alongside innovative approaches to lighting. Our Zumtobel, Thorn and TridonicAtco brands consistently invest in innovative technologies: our aim is to develop intelligent lighting solutions that optimise energy use, for example by using daylight-based control and presence detectors, or through appropriate lighting design. This approach makes it possible for us to save 80 per cent of energy – while improving the quality of light at the same time. The fact is that apart from energy efficiency, the lighting quality has an important part to play in terms of people's safety and performance, and also enhances their well-being.

As well as developing energy-efficient products and systems, we are concerned to make our commitment to sustainability perceptible at a higher level. Hence we have joined forces with the Aedes Architektur Forum in Berlin to set up the Zumtobel Group Award for more sustainability and humanity in the built environment. Our close co-operation with leading architects, engineers and lighting designers has shown us that visionary solutions drawn from architecture and town planning can make an important contribution to reducing global energy use and to improving the quality of life in general.

The award enables us to stimulate new concepts and developments in the built environment and to make the public aware of them. One particularly important aspect of the prize is to combine energy efficiency with human need. The work submitted for the first Zumtobel Group Award has made it clear how many problems relating to the development, use and saving of resources, to avoiding natural disasters, and also to education and training are to be found in a whole variety of world regions. These projects have shown very clearly where good solutions in architecture, regional planning and engineering have to start if they are to provide sustainable development prospects for the people involved.

I am delighted that, as well as awarding the prize, we have been able to use a touring exhibition and this publication to draw public attention to our project. We hope that the Zumtobel Group Award has made it possible for us to boost sustainable, humane design for our environment. We will continue our commitment in this spirit, and announce the next Zumtobel Group Award in the coming year.

Karl Sevelda

Managing Board, Raiffeisen Zentralbank
Österreich AG

It is a great honour for the Raiffeisen Zentralbank Österreich (RZB) to be the main sponsor of the Zumtobel Group Award for Sustainability and Humanity in the Built Environment including the publication at hand. We have supported culture and the arts as a direct contribution to society over the last years. This is part of our lived responsibility, understanding business as being based on trust and ethical values.

Riders On the Storm. Into This House We're Born and Into This World We're Thrown

by Lukas Feireiss

Lukas Feireiss is a teacher, writer and curator deeply involved in the discussion and mediation of architecture beyond its disciplinary boundaries.

"The storm is master. Man, as a ball, is tossed twixt winds and billows."

Friedrich Schiller

In Walt Disney's 1935 cartoon *The Band Concert*, a little orchestra brilliantly defies wind and weather in a perform-ance of Rossini's William Tell overture. A tornado is appar-ently conjured up by the storm portrayed in the second part of the overture. It drags entire houses in its wake, drives the audience away and whirls the whole orchestra and their stage through the air. Even this was not enough to stop the musi-cians playing. As conductor in the eye of the storm, Mickey Mouse, in a state of blind self-obsession, pushes the orches-tra on to the tempestuous end, accompanied by drum-rolls regardless of the stormy threat. Riders on the Storm. Bravo!

Our behaviour in the face of incipient massive change in all spheres of our life caused by natural forces rebelling at climate change is, to a certain extent, comparable with the behaviour of Mickey Mouse and his friends. We see the storm coming, we are actually making it happen, and when it hits us we orchestrate the soundtrack of our own rise and fall in fatalistic surrender.

I   Globally Green

"Climate chaos is becoming the new fashion."

Bruce Sterling

For some time now, all the lights have seemed to be on green. A new sense of global awareness of our natural envi-ronment's vulnerability, demanding that we pursue active change, has been granted a clear run. Climate change and sustainability are on everyone's lips, and have thus become media-friendly – from sober, ecological and political spe-cialist publications down to the high-gloss format of design, trend and lifestyle magazines. If the environmental movement carried the stigma of naive do-goodery in previous decades, expressed in an alternative lifestyle and its very own aesthetic, the movement has now developed into a global trend. An ardent, at times even aggressive alarmism, thereby marks the argument. Now or never seems to be the cry. The former US vice-president Al Gore has become a trademark of the new green movement with his *Inconvenient Truth*, Leonardo di Caprio adds fuel in the *11th Hour*, Brad Pitt promotes architecture competitions to boost ecological and sustainable reconstruc-tion for the New Orleans district Lower Ninth Ward, laid to waste by hurricane Katrina, and a gigantic live concert staged simultaneously on seven continents attracts world-wide atten-tion to the subject of global warming. Even the notoriously politically incorrect *Simpsons* are devoting themselves to a satiri-cal parody of climate change in their first feature film.

Ultimately, scientists have pushed this process forward with the insight that mankind is helping to cause global warm-ing and its devastating consequences. Signs that such warming really is taking place are steadily increasing as the sets of statis-tics get longer and longer, we understand the climate system better, and computer models are refined. In the last twenty years, proof that the human race must share responsibility for the development is accumulating inexorably. In the scientific community, the feeling that climate change is indeed taking place on a hitherto unprecedented scale has now strength-ened into a certainty. Surely the boundaries between facts and speculation are pretty fluid here. But what we can now offer is what is known as cumulative evidence: hundreds of pieces of mosaic producing a complete picture.

Politics and economics also seem to be drawing conclu-sions from this. October 2006 saw the report by the former world banker Sir Nicholas Stern on *The Economics of Climate Change*, in which he quantified the so-called consequential costs of climate change. This started a year that seemed to be concerned with climate protection throughout. The climate report published by the UN in February 2007 presented us with alarming scenarios, and in March the EU heads of state and government agreed to a 20 per cent reduction of carbon dioxide emissions by 2020. In May, another publication, the *World Climate Report*, discussed the economic consequences of global warming. And the supranational meeting of the G8 states in Heiligendamm in June 2007 was entirely dominated by climate change. In late September, the UN plenary session in New York also carried a torch for climate protection. A month later the Nobel Peace Prize was awarded to the IPCC (Intergovernmental Commission on Climate Change) and to Al Gore and in December 2007 the World Climate Conference was held on the island of Bali, and this again sounded a warning against doing nothing about climate protection.

It is a start, but the mills of politics grind slowly. Yet one of the greatest obstacles to mobilising against climate change, is that it becomes a cliché even before it has been properly understood.

II   Nature Calls

"I don't need a weatherman to know which way the wind blows."

Bob Dylan

The fact that the polar icecaps are melting and mountain glaciers receding at an enormous speed, coral reefs are dying out because of higher water temperatures and world sea levels are rising inexorably can not be ignored The deserts are getting larger with increasing speed, which causes severe famine. Fierce storms and heat waves are accumulating to presage even greater

natural disasters if oil and coal continue to be used as energy sources at the present rate. The destruction of the natural bases for our lives and the consequences of this represents one of the greatest challenges for the 21st century. Given the fact that none of this is new, but has been debated for a long time, we have to wonder whether fresh disasters really are needed to cause a genuine change in our approach? Unfortunately history teaches us that human beings really are not long-term planners, but respond almost exclusively to crises.

We have to face the fact that we were being warned about the incalculable climatic consequence of the greenhouse effect since the 1970s. The death of forests, the growing hole in the ozone layer, dwindling rain forests and oil pollution caused by tankers were major themes that then encouraged a lot of people to join the environmental movement. But over ten years of increasing CO_2 emissions worldwide have passed even since the Kyoto negotiations. It is only now that this information seems to have been taken on board, i.e. grasped in terms of its significance and implications. People are presently occupied in changing the space they live in comprehensibly and lastingly. An increasing world population of six billion people at the time of writing, with hitherto unknown technical abilities, is massively affecting global nature. Civilisation has become a force of nature in its own right, causing far-reaching changes in the ecosystem — changes that also affect our lives and those of future generations.

III   Live Earth

"Geologists have a saying – rocks remember."

Neil Armstrong

The present situation is most appositely described by the joke about the two planets who meet again in space after a long time and ask each other how they are getting on. "You don't look too good!" says one to the other. The other planet replies: "No, I'm not doing too well, I've got *homo sapiens*." The first replies: "Don't worry about it, I had that once, but it will pass!" Jokes always contain a grain of truth in their exaggerated presentation of a situation. And even more, the truth is often the great joke itself! But one thing is clear at any rate: we are playing for our earth, and the stakes are high!

Against this background, this book is devoting itself to the highly topical subject of ecological change caused, among other things, by man's intervention into the existing ecosystem. It is doing this from the point of view of people who create buildings, who confront the natural world with the built world. Given the fact that building almost always involves intervening in a natural environment in favour of a built environment, and over and above this, about forty per cent of energy consumption world-wide is due within the building sphere, so any construction project, however small, proves to be a piece of built responsibility. It does not just serve the people who live in it, but also has to deal carefully with the environment and with human resources.

Here we are dealing with ecology, the science of how living creatures relate to each other and to their environment. In terms of sustainability, it asks how anthropogenous ecosystems, i.e. structures of connections and effects (such as architecture and the city, for example) created or changed by man, behave in terms of their natural environment or their habitat, and vice versa. So as far as the built environment is concerned, it is not just architects, town planners and engineers who have to address the capacity of the dramatically changing worlds we live in to face the future, but actually the whole of mankind. Hence the present publication, *Architecture of Change*, introduces innovative architecture and research projects that address the challenges of environmental friendliness in the built environment through a combination of creativity, scientific insight, technological innovation, commitment to society and

social responsibility, and at the same time discusses associated open questions critically with internationally acclaimed experts from the worlds of architecture, art, science, economics and politics.

The fact is, that there is one thing that ecological investigations have been able to show us: there is no future in isolation. Mankind can simply not create an autonomous, closed system for the race to live in. As a system of this kind always has to rely on natural cycles and resources, it also needs a variety of different approaches and positions in order to deal with subject matter as complex as sustainability and humanity in the built environment.

It is not this publication's function to simply offer solutions to these difficult questions that affect us all, but nevertheless everyone involved has an interest in creating space for reflection, exchanging ideas and critical analysis, and in introducing constructive projects and suggestions for action that admit prospects and future utopias. The works collected here want to attract attention to the urgent questions and problems of our day and to bring about positive change.

IV   Sustainability and Humanity in the Built Environment

"If you strip away all the ego and all the design theory and all the hype, all we do is provide shelter and if you can't do that you can't call yourself an architect."
Cameron Sinclair

The wide-ranging nature of the subject matter automatically raises the question of whether *sustainability* and *humanity* in the *built environment* can anyway be communicated appropriately as a subject for argument. It seems to involve an infinite number of concerns relating to public life and human activity. But can these concepts gain the public ear at all within such a wide-ranging framework? Without even starting to address these questions, it is at least possible to indicate a way through this multidimensional set of problems by questioning the individual concepts critically. Taking them back to their conceptual origins could well help us to understand here.

> *sustain [origin: 1250–1300; ME suste(i)nen < AF sustenir, OF < L sustinére to uphold, equiv. to sus- sus + -tinére, comb. form of tenére to hold]*

Even in the early 20th century, all that was communicated in the context of sustainability were concerns relating to forestry and later to agriculture; in the latter case in relation to looking at over-cultivation of fertile soil. People realized that ruthless exploitation of the soil also had economic disadvantages, as after a few years formerly fertile arable land became irreversibly infertile.

The area covered by the concept of sustainability was massively extended when the Club of Rome published its 1972 report *The Limits of Growth*. This now went beyond agriculture and forestry to cover the ecology of the earth as a whole. The authors, Dennis Meadows et al., developed several more or less gloomy future scenarios in respect of the five basic phenomena they had researched: population, food production, industrialisation, environmental pollution and the exploitation of raw materials. To sum up: only immediate, far-reaching environmental protection and birth control measures could sustain the world population's long-term welfare.

The social component in global ecological terms of sustainability-related matters discussed in this study was explicitly mentioned in the World Commission on Environment and Development's 1987 *Brundtland Report*. This deals above all with the distribution of world resources.

Essentially the report defines sustainable development as an attempt to meet the needs of the present without putting future generations at risk of not being able to meet their needs. The Brundtland report introduced the concept of sustainability into global ecology debates that still determines the course of such debates in the present day. The term implies much more than notions like environment-friendly or ecologically meaningful. First of all, it points the discussion towards generational problems in using global resources. Given that sustainability was now directed not just at ecological and social measures, this subject, previously confined to environmental ecology, was extended to cover social concerns. This report also formed the basis for the UN Conference on Environment and Development in Rio de Janeiro in 1992 and all other meetings in which sustainability in the global context becomes the key concept in a directive to which associations of states had to commit.

It is easy, given its conserving and obtaining character, to see the concept of sustainability wrongly in this context as a somewhat static and preservative element that resists change of any kind. Wide of the mark! Sustainability also always covers a system's ability to reproduce itself under constantly changing conditions. Here sustainability denotes the ability to develop further, and this can include changes of location as well as forms and ways of functioning that change in the course of time. This also means that sustainability cannot reach a final condition, it is simply one element within a dynamic equilibrium.

> *human [c.1250, from M.Fr. humain "of or belonging to man," from L. humanus, probably related to homo (gen. hominis) "man," and to humus "earth," on notion of "earthly beings," as opposed to the gods (cf. Heb. adam "man," from adamah "ground")]*

In the first place, humanity means the community of all men, mankind as such. Secondly this is associated with the fundamental condition and existential quality of being human, the *conditio humana*, the nature of man. But over and above this, humanity also includes the quality of compassion and human solidarity.

When examining the concept more closely, a surprising semantic stratum comes to light. If the concept is followed back to its etymological origins, then another double meaning emerges that is interesting in our context. As described previously in all facets, man as a species is a primary presence in the concept of humanity. It is not just the nature of man in all his complexity that is under discussion, but also his preferred home, the earth. The Latin word *humanus* is related not just to *homo*, "human being", but also to *humus*, "earth". Man is not to be seen as an autonomous factor, as he is connected to the earth existentially and by name as an earthly being. Our very nature is anchored in the soil, as it were. Nomen ist omen. So whenever we talk about humanity, we are also talking about our original environment, the earth, without which we would not exist.

> *environ [origin: 1300–50; ME environouen < OF environner,*
> *deriv. of environ around (en en + viron a circle; vir(er) to turn,*
> *veer + -on n. suffix)]*

Environment is a general term for the world about us, in its different contexts. It appears as a complex network of all the influences affecting nature and the individual, whether they are of social, cultural, political, economic or ecological nature.

But the built environment, which is the particular province of this book, has always drawn a clear dividing line between itself and its counterpart, the natural environment. From the outset, the fundamental aim of architecture has always been to guarantee human beings protection and shelter from a whole variety of dangers and threats. This creates an artificial space that is different from natural space. To a certain extent this places architecture, as a practice that creates autonomous environments, in opposition with the nature that surrounds it. Architecture needs this demarcation in order to constitute itself. This assertion is certainly true of Modernist architecture, which did a great deal to shape the architectural appearance of the first half of the 20th century and well beyond with its austere, functionalistic approach. With its preference for new industrial technologies, it produced a kind of architecture that invested everything in existing independently of nature, culminating characteristically in Le Corbusier's description of a building as a "machine for living".

Over the past fifty years people have increasingly recognised that this mechanical demarcation line did not seem sustainable when designing our modern environment and the lifestyle it brings with it and encourages. Constructing and maintaining these structures destroys resources more rapidly than natural systems can produce them, above all when these natural systems are being damaged by poisonous substances at the same time. Generally speaking, the building industry therefore contributes to the destruction of the natural environment, and it does this at considerable speed. We have only to be clear that at the beginning of the 20th century there were sixteen cities with one million inhabitants, and now there are almost four hundred on this scale, taking in more and more waves of inhabitants. And the trend is rising!

This points us towards the fields of architecture and town planning, and is not just a challenge to act but almost a provocation to do so. Certainly a large number of guidelines have already been laid down for extending the process of designing building projects and general conditions for them in such a way that effects on the environment are taken into consideration as well. But it continues to prove difficult to find standards of sustainability that are objective and applicable all over the world. For example, something that seems to be a revolution in sustainable building in the United States at the moment may have been standard practice in Europe for decades. And the ecological efficiency of a building cannot be calculated by figures alone. The use of resources for producing and constructing a building out of nothing but straw and clay in a developing country is not comparable with building an 18-storey skyscraper within a dense urban fabric, even if the latter stands out for a highly ingenious ecological concept. On the other hand, given that half the world's population lives in cities today, a large-scale architectural project in an urban context, like the aforementioned skyscraper, has much more far-reaching influence in terms of global warming and questions of sustainability.

It is a difficult state of affairs. One positive example, and perhaps the best known of all the units of measurement, is the *ecological footprint* devised by Mathis Wackernagel and William E. Rees. This identifies the area of the earth needed to make a person's lifestyle and standard of living viable in the long term while present production conditions continue. But if mathematical assessments of this kind are applied on a global scale we are faced with an alarming conclusion: if everyone in the world lived the life of the highly developed conurbations, then we would need the equivalent of three to seven planets earth to sustain this lifestyle. Good night and good luck!

Given these disturbing prospects, what has architecture to offer in addressing this urgent set of global problems? What can design processes contribute to a better world? And how can the natural and the built environment be brought into harmony?

"Good architecture comes from good architects. Great architecture has to come from a client."
Thom Mayne

This book tries to approach these questions in various different ways. Intellectual and aesthetic reflection in addressing nature and the environment is inherent in all the pieces of work and positions presented here. It rapidly becomes clear that it has long been impossible for a single profession to deal with creating accomplished architecture in all its complexity, diversity and multifunctionality. Architects see themselves facing new challenges and responsibilities today that go well beyond their discipline's horizon of experience. If these challenges are to be met, then an integrative approach must be taken to break down the boundaries between architecture and other spheres of knowledge. The key to acquiring new insights is being able to see and think out of the box.

About forty projects from the sphere of architecture are presented here, and now is also the moment to give credit to the numerous authors from a whole variety of disciplinary backgrounds who have considerably enhanced the quality of this publication with their critical contributions. We are particularly grateful to Saskia Sassen, Lynd Professor of Sociology at Columbia University, for her essay. Klaus Töpfer the former Executive Director of the United Nations Environment Programme and Yung Ho Chang, Director of the Department of Architecture at the Massachusetts Institute of Technology in Boston have enriched the content of the publication as a whole with their interviews. Thanks also go in this context to Hans-Jürgen Commerell and Friedrich von Borries, without whose co-operation the selection of works we have made here would not have come about. In addition, our sincere thanks go to Matthew Petersen, CEO and President of Global Green, Leon van Schaik, Professor of Innovation at the RMIT University in Australia and to the architects Ken Yeang and William McDonough, distinguished because of their exemplary role in the sphere of ecological design, for being ready to grace *Architecture of Change* with their valuable and critical essays. The book does not thrive only on its practical architectural and research projects and sound theoretical writing, but also to a great extent on the artistic contributions framing the book, which act to some extent here as wilful mediators at the interface between science, technology, culture and nature.

All these contributions come together in their inspiring bandwidth to create a new picture of sustainable thinking and action that takes our built environment as an example of how to make a problem into a concrete possibility, opening up a representative insight into the current state of development in this field. Here it quickly becomes clear that within a generation, sustainable architecture has succeeded in moving away from its decades of being an outsider and into the mainstream, and is now having a lasting influence on even the current artistic avant-garde. The eco-banality of its outward appearance has now given way to aesthetically demanding design concepts. Indeed it almost seems that the ecological performance of buildings is becoming the new architectural aesthetic. So sustainability is acquiring a new aesthetic dimension in contemporary architecture beyond its pragmatic and ethical relevance.

The projects in this book are brought together under three thematic headings. They are to be seen as exemplary for the development described, as environmentally aware concepts form an integral component of their outstanding architectural formal language. They are all distinguished by their flexible and holistic approach throughout the whole planning, design and construction processes. Even though

the categories selected demarcate the projects from each other, the projects remain essentially open, even inviting exchanges of ideas.

The first chapter, *Efficiency in the Everyday*, looks at realised and unrealised projects that can be categorised by their sustainable intervention into everyday urban and rural life. Family houses in Germany, Australia and England by Werner Sobek, Paul Morgan or Youmeheshe are considered alongside schools by Grüntuch Ernst, SMC Alsop or Ingenhoven Architekten, but so is experimental work by practices like Ecosistem Urbano and the Urban-Think Tank, who address the infrastructure of problem urban areas.

The *Aesthetics of Performance* chapter illustrates the creative richness of contemporary architecture whose appearance is shaped by ideas on ecological performance. The range extends from straw buildings in Austria to hand-made clay structures in Bangladesh and brick buildings at the foot of the Himalayas, and then on to very modern research institutions and skyscrapers in the USA, Australia, Germany and China. Younger architects like Anna Herringer and Eike Roswag or KOL/MAC feature alongside internationally successful architecture practices such as that of the Pritzker Prize winner Thom Mayne of Morphosis in Los Angeles or Steven Holl in New York. Outstanding buildings by Sauerbruch Hutton, Rafael Vinoly, Mario Cucinella and many others can be found.

The concluding chapter, *Didactics of Engagement*, discusses the work of a whole variety of organisations, institutions and individual architects who have made an exemplary commitment to improving the environment we live in through their world-wide engagement in architecture and urban development. The spheres documented here range from Open Source Internet platforms to community projects in developing countries, experimental approaches to flood protection and alternative solar power stations. Projects by

Architecture for Humanity, Engineers without Borders, Auburn Universtiy's Rural Studio and MIT's SENSEable City Laboratory appear alongside those by Miralles Tagliabue, Diébédo Francis Kéré and Schlaich Bergermann Solar, to name but some.

The kaleidoscopic spectrum of motivations lying behind the work presented in *Architecture of Change* presents an image of the wealth of creative ideas for developing spatial possibilities in the sustainability sphere and humanity in the built environment. They all make their contribution to maintaining and continuously renewing our environment. When choosing projects from Africa, Australia, Asia, Europe and America, the aim was to make the wide-ranging scope of the activities clear and to show particularly successful examples.

VI   Deeper Shades of Green

"Change is the law of life. And those who look only to the past or present are certain to miss the future."

John F. Kennedy

Though the work presented here is motivating and inspiring, the sustainability debate is far more complicated. Green buildings, projects and concepts that have a less negative effect on our environment, or even represent zero energy concepts, do not solve the urgent problem of climate change by a long run. Architecture is only one link in the chain. There is much more at stake.

Society can scarcely foresee the scale of the social and political effects of climate change. It is difficult for people to assess climate change dispassionately because it has far-reaching political and economic consequences and because it is caused precisely by the processes that make our civilisation success-

ful. Since the start of the Industrial Revolution in the late 18th century, the unchecked use of fossil fuels and the emissions of greenhouse gases associated with them has meant that the atmosphere of our planet has become warmer. The prevailing lifestyle and economic behaviour incurred ecological debts – relating to the future, to the earth's non-renewable resources, to biodiversity and to the majority of people in underdeveloped countries. This lifestyle is maintained at their expense, at the expense of future generations, at the expense of the planet's ability to survive. While the industrialised countries owe their prosperity to historical greenhouse gas emissions – economic growth used to be in direct proportion to the increasing use of fossil energy -, the developing and newly industrialised countries have contributed almost nothing to this problem. Additionally, they are also worst hit by the consequences of climate change. We have only to remember that at the time of writing one fifth of the world, namely the industrialised nations, use four-fifths of global resources. Massive commercial interests, above all in the large industrialised countries, are behind the developments that are throwing the earth and its climate increasingly off balance. On the other hand, rapid economic development in the newly industrialised countries makes it impossible to divest them of all responsibility.

The great challenge is to break the causal chain of economic development and energy consumption, which would need nothing less than a new industrial revolution. This requires the industrialised countries to be reconstructed as societies with sustainable economies. And then the newly industrialised and developing countries must be helped to keep to the sustainability path as they strive for prosperity.

Reform of this kind will make a profound impact on the economic structure of the nation states, will burden them with expenses in the billions, but also opens up opportunities for growth. In any case it is always about the economy, about the distribution of resources, about spaces available for decision and design and about social hierarchies. Predictions like those made by the Geneva Climate Commission assert that in a hundred years most countries will have to spend a large proportion of their gross domestic product on repairing climate-related damage and adjustment measures. On a global scale, says the Stern's report, the proportions are even more dramatic, and are estimated at up to twenty per cent of global economic performance unless policies change rapidly.

The challenges we face in trying to limit damage and adjust to climate change and that will affect practically every sphere of our lives are unprecedented, but not insurmountable. There is a great deal to be done and the path to global agreements, for example in relation to CO2 emissions, remains thorny. Nevertheless, we must be clear about the fact that delays will only push future costs even higher.

VII   Business as Usual

"I've never turned over a fig leaf yet that didn't have a price tag on the other side"

Saul Bellow

As monetary values are a driving force behind world politics, and a mere environmental disaster is far less convincing than a possible world economic crisis, there actually is a hope that the numerous warnings will bear fruit. Money makes the world go round.

Over and above this, ecology has become an important marketing instrument. Environmental issues have found their way on to the capitalist agenda. 'Organic' or 'eco' labels have become an economic factor with market relevance. People talk about 'green glamour', 'eco-chic' and 'ecological correctness' as contributions to sustaining the planet. Investment banks are pouring billions into earning money from eco-firms in the future. Anyone offering ecological products or producing them ecologically is creating added value in the hotly disputed consumer market.

It certainly seems dubious when car firms appear as official sponsors for global concerts in aid of climate protection, when fast food concerns, the ultimate symbol of the throw-away society and globalisation, distribute free teaching material on the subject of the environment in campaigns directed particularly at children and young people, when aircraft manufacturers place an image of a dolphin or a lush area of green woodland in the outline of their new giant jumbo and add the words 'greener' and 'cleaner', and when thinking about the *Inconvenient Truth* of climate change is conducted almost exclusively while looking out of the windows of limousines and private jets.

Even if these examples of drum-rolls in environment politics represent extremes, it is certainly justifiable to ask whether we really need the combination of healthy enterprise and market-oriented self-interest to bring about the necessary change? However hypocritical this may sound against the background of the necessity for change, the economic profitability of acting ecologically is far more attractive than the prospect of an incipient climate disaster.

VIII   State of Mind

"When all is said and done, more is said than done."

Groucho Marx

So where do we ourselves actually stand in the face of climate change? How are we prepared to accept restrictions and change? The majority of people still do very little. Yet this should not make them feel guilty because a real change in climate change is not about guilt and expiation. On the contrary, mistakes and errors are natural milestones in the search for new solutions; they show us what we have overlooked and what we could do better and more intelligently.

We now have both the technology and the knowledge to make considerable improvements. But even if our everyday lives were to become more sustainable through the use of the latest technologies or the application of natural regulation mechanisms, it is still our individual behaviour and our readiness to adapt that will effect a change. And this does not just mean switching to products that damage the environment less. This is often just a superficial measure. We need to rethink on the cultural plane, because social conventions in each particular cultural context are more important than products as such.

But to do this, again needs more than just our personal involvement. Fundamental changes to transport, and to energy and other systems will all require long-term visions, leadership, co-operation, innovation and investment by companies and the authorities at all levels. It is therefore just as important to commit the state as to increase the proportion of our personal efforts.

Given the fact that in coming years the subject of the environment will probably put everything else in the shade, it is important that much-mentioned climate change should at the same time introduce a profound change of awareness. Here the current discussion circles rightly around 'efficiency', 'sufficiency' and 'structural reform', i.e. in the same order, the fact that the same solutions are found while consuming fewer resources, that consumption is restricted and that the way our society meets its needs has to undergo fundamental change. This sounds like saving and going without. The years of plenty are over! But what really is needed today is not so much rhetoric about minimisation and cutting back, but a new sense of forward-looking ecological intelligence that suc-

cessfully learns from nature. Positive guidelines have to be formulated that illustrate vividly what we can achieve. Hope has always been a more successful motivator than fear.

IX   The Day After Tomorrow

"What is not started today is never finished tomorrow."
Johann Wolfgang von Goethe

Naturally, every new beginning first needs the courage to face the facts and the will to solve the problems it raises. But even more, it needs the strength to define a target and a commitment to meeting it.

The fact is, that for decades now we have been rather like the fool sawing at the branch he is sitting on and imagining anyone who warns him about the inevitable fall to be a soothsayer and clairvoyant. Today, joke and reality are much the same. The branch we are sawing away at is our environment. And the joke is on us!

Literature:
- Joseph E. Aldy and Robert N. Stavins, ed., (2007) *Architectures of Agreement. Addressing Global Climate Change in the Post-Kyoto World* Cambridge: Cambridge University Press
- Max Andrews, ed. (2006) *Land, Art. A Cultural Ecology Handbook* Manchester: Royal Society for the Encouragement of Arts, Manufactures & Commerce
- William R. Blackburn (2007) *The Sustainablity Handbook. The Complete Management Guide to Achieving Social, Economic and Environmental Responsibility* London:Earthscan Ltd.
- Kirstin Dow and Thomas E. Downing, ed. (2007) *The Atlas of Climate Change: Mapping the World's Greatest Challenge* London: Earthscan Ltd.
- Tim Flannery (2006) *The Weather Makers: How Man is Changing the Climate and What It Means for Life on Earth* London: Atlantic Monthly Press
- Sabine Himmelsbach and Yvonne Volkart, ed. (2007) *Ecomedia. Ecological Strategies in Today's Art* Ostfildern: Hatje Cantz
- Intergovernmental Panel on Climate Change, Climate Change 2007 (2007) *The Physical Science Basis* Cambridge: Cambridge University Press
- Intergovernmental Panel on Climate Change, Climate Change 2007 (2008) *Mitigation of Climate Change* Cambridge: Cambridge University Press
- Elizabeth Kolbert (2006) *Field Notes From a Catastrophe. Man, Nature and Climate Change* Bloomsbury: Bloomsbury USA
- Le Monde diplomatique (2006) *Atlas der Globalisierung. Die neuen Daten und Fakten zur Lage der Welt* Berlin: Taz
- Donella H Meadows and Dennis Meadows, ed. (1972) *The Limits of Growth: A Report for the Club of Rome's Project on the Predicament of Mankind* New York: Universe Pub.
- Donella H Meadows, Dennis Meadows and Jorgen Randers, ed. (2004) *The Limits of Growth: The 30-Year Update* White River: Chelsea Green Publishing Company
- Nicholas Stern (2007) *The Economics of Climate Change. The Stern Review* Cambridge: Cambridge University Press
- Grui Bang Softing, Gerorge Benneh, ed. (1998) *The Brundtland Commission's Report: 10 Years* Sentrum: Aschehoug AS
- Warner Troyer, Preserving our World (1990) *A Consumer's Guide to the Brundtland Report* Richmond Hill: Firefly Books Ltd.

Cities: At the Heart of Our Environmental Future

by Saskia Sassen

Saskia Sassen is Lynd Professor of
Sociology at Columbia University and
Member of The Committee of Global
Thought, Columbia University.

The massive processes of urbanisation under way today are inevitably at the centre of the environmental future. Yet they have largely not been at the centre of environmental research. It is through cities and vast urban agglomerations that humankind is increasingly present in the world and through which it mediates its relation to the various stocks and flows of environmental capital. The urban hinterland, once a mostly confined geographic zone, is today a global hinterland. This represents a radical transformation in the relation between humans and the rest of the planet.

Having a large number of cities with multi-million populations is a new condition in our history, as is the urbanisation of over half the people in the world. Urban agglomerations are today the engines of consumption of the world's environment: they occupy only two per cent of the world's land surface, but use over 75 per cent of the world's resources. Humans now consume nearly half of the world's total photosynthetic capacity, and cities are the major factor in this. Cities in the North require an average of four to five hectares of ecologically productive land per inhabitant. Further, much economic activity that takes place outside cities is geared towards cities. With the expansion of the global economy, we have raised our capability to annex growing portions of the world to support a limited number of industries and places. Cities also have a pronounced effect on traditional rural economies and their long-standing cultural adaptation to biological diversity. Rural populations increasingly become consumers of products produced in the industrial economy, one much less sensitive to biological diversity. The rural condition has evolved into a new system of social relations, one that does not work with biodiversity. These developments all signal that the urban condition is a major factor in any environmental future.

Through this enormously distinctive presence that is urbanisation, we are changing a growing range of ecological systems from the climate to species diversity and ocean purity and we are creating new environmental conditions of heat islands, desertification, and water pollution. We have entered a new phase in human ecological history. For the first time humankind is the major ecological factor on the planet, in a way it was not in the past. Massive urbanisation over the last few decades has created a set of global ecological conditions never seen before. But is it urbanisation per se or the particular types of urban systems and industrial processes, that we have instituted? That is to say, are these global ecological conditions the result of urban agglomeration and density or are they the result of the urban systems for transport, waste disposal, heating and cooling, food provision, and the industrial process through which we extract, grow, make, package, distribute, and dispose of all the foods and services we use?

We can begin by conceptualising the urban condition as a socio-ecological system in that it creates a whole new set of interrelations between, on the one hand, its constructed features and material practices and, on the other, various ecological systems. In the current stage, the systemic characteristics of this inter-relation are mostly in the form of environmental damage. A growing number of researchers today are calling for the need to use and build upon those features of cities that can make cities into a socio-ecological system with positive outcomes. Specific features of cities with such positive potential are economies of scale, density and the associated potential for greater efficiency in resource use and lower priced options, and dense networks of communication that can serve as facilitators to institute new practices. More theoretically, one can say that in so far as cities are constituted through various processes that produce space, time, place and nature, cities also contain the transformative possibilities embedded in these same processes.

Because they are at the centre of the environmental future, urbanisation and the city also must be understood and used as potentially containing the solutions to many of these

This essay is based on a large project, one of the volumes (Volume on Human Settlement) of the 14-volume Encyclopedia for Life-World Systems, prepared for Unesco and EOLSS (Oxford, 2005). In the larger volume from which this is drawn, we opted to include a large number of very specific studies by researchers and by activists (some of whom never write! But act) from many different parts of the world and diverse disciplinary backgrounds. We kept general overviews to a minimum because they inevitably need to neutralise the variety and specificity evident across the world. We have over seventy case studies by authors from 30 different countries. We have put enormous weight on the specific instantiations of general dynamics.

↘ | Geographies of Environmental Accountability.
Source: Based on Rio Tinto Sassen and Schroeder "Cities and Global Warming" 2007 (In Preparation), Urban Age, LSE, Cities Program

problems. As has been much documented, cities have long been sites for innovation and for developing and instituting complex physical and organisational systems. It is within the complexity of the city that we must find the solutions to much environmental damage and the formulas for reconfiguring the socio-ecological system that is urbanisation. Cities contain the networks and information loops that may facilitate communicating, informing, and persuading households, governments, and firms to support and participate in environmentally sensitive programs and in radically transformative institution building.

Urban systems also entail systems of social relations that support the current configuration. Beyond adoption of practices such as waste recycling, it will take a change in this system of social relations itself to achieve greater environmental sensitivity and efficiency. For instance, a crucial issue is the massive investment around the world promoting large projects that damage the environment. Deforestation and construction of large dams are perhaps among the best known cases. The scale and the increasingly global and private character of these investments suggest that citizens, governments, NGOs, all lack the power to alter these investment patterns.

But there are possibilities for acting on these deeply damaging economic operations. The geography of economic globalisation is strategic rather than all-encompassing and this is especially so when it comes to the managing, coordinating, servicing and financing of global economic operations. The fact that it is strategic, is significant for a discussion about the possibilities of regulating and governing the global economy. There are sites in this strategic geography, most importantly global cities, where the density of economic transactions and top-level management functions come together and represent a strategic geography of decision-making. We can see this also as a strategic geography for demanding accountability about environmental damage. It is precisely because the global

economic system is characterised by enormous concentration of power in a limited number of large multinational corporations and global financial markets that makes for concentrated (rather than widely dispersed) sites for accountability and for changing investment criteria. This leaves out a whole range of less central and powerful economic actors responsible for much environmental damage, but are more likely to be controllable through national level regulatory interventions.

A crucial issue raised by all the above, is the question of the scales at which damage is produced and intervention or change should occur. These may in turn differ from the levels and sites for responsibility and accountability. The city is, in this regard, an enormously complex entity. Cities are multi-scalar systems where many of the environmental dynamics that concern us are constituted and in turn constitute what we call the city, and where different policy levels, from the supra- to the sub-national, get implemented. Further, specific networks of mostly global cities, also constitute a key component of the global scale and hence can be thought of as a network of sites for accountability of global economic actors.

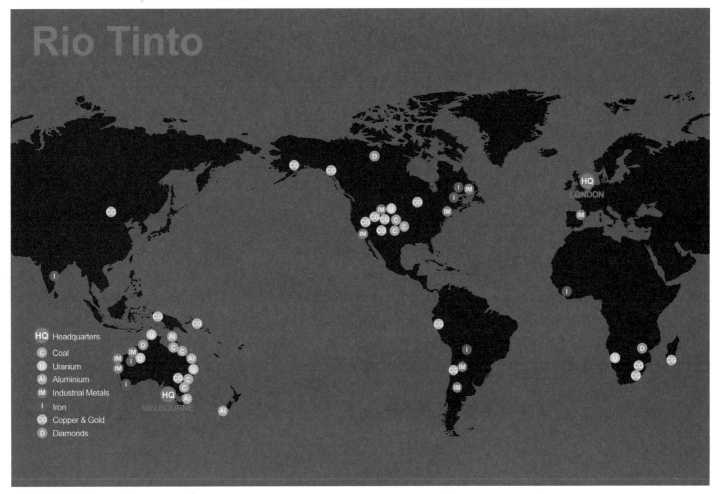

Rio Tinto

HQ Headquarters
C   Coal
U   Uranium
Al Aluminium
IM Industrial Metals
I   Iron
CG Copper & Gold
D   Diamonds

Because cities bring together our economic, political, cultural, ideological, and technical systems and practices, the treatment of the subject demands multiple forms of knowledge. Dealing with the question of the environment in the context of cities and rural-urban interactions requires an extraordinary mix of disciplines. Further, because we are dealing with an enormous variety of political and economic systems, levels of wealth and power, cultural understandings and ideological convictions, it is necessary to bring in analyses that represent many of these differences. It is not simply a question of scientific knowledge and shared theoretical understandings.

This complexity and variety assume even more weight when we consider that the question of urban sustainability requires engaging the legal systems and profit logics that underlie and enable many of the environmentally damaging aspects of our societies. The question of urban sustainability cannot be reduced to modest interventions that leave these major systems untouched. And the actual features of these systems vary across countries and across the North-South divide. While in some environmental themes examined in various volumes it is indeed possible to confine the treatment of the subject to scientific knowledge, this is not the

case when dealing with human settlements. When it comes to cities, non-scientific elements are a crucial part of the picture: questions of power, of poverty and inequality, ideology and cultural preferences, are all part of the question and the answer. Questions of policy and proactive engagement possibilities are a critical dimension of treatments of urban sustainability, whether they involve asking people to support garbage recycling or demanding accountability from major global corporations known to have environmentally damaging production processes.

01

Efficiency
in the
Everyday

This chapter looks at realised and unrealised projects that can be categorised by their sustainable intervention into everyday urban and rural life. All these contributions come together in their inspiring bandwidth to create a new picture of sustainable thinking and action that takes our built environment as an example of how to make a problem into a concrete possibility, opening up a representative insight into the current state of development in this field.

Rethinking Architecture: Creating Climate Solutions That Work for Urban Centres and Low-Income Communities

by Matt Petersen

Matt Petersen is Global Green USA's President and CEO.

More than half of humanity lives in cities and the percentage of urban dwellers among the world's population increases every day. Given that 40 per cent of our energy use and global warming-inducing greenhouse gas emissions result from the construction and operations of buildings (and 60 per cent to 70 per cent of all electricity use), it is clear that the future of our urban centres and the global environment are inextricably linked.

Further, our cities are at threat from global warming, particularly cities in coastal regions. The overwhelming and increasing scientific consensus shows that global warming is causing sea levels to rise and increasing storm intensity while worsening erosion and flooding. The United Nations' Intergovernmental Panel on Climate Change (IPCC) recently reported that 'many millions more people are projected to be flooded every year due to sea-level rise by the 2080s.

Unfortunately, reports released after the IPCC report was finalised indicate that sea-level rise could be much worse than predicted, given the accelerated melting of Greenland and Antarctica. While such developments may appear distant for now, their impact will one day be felt hardest in cities, with poor citizens in low-lying flood areas suffering the most.

Any effective response to climate change must, of course, involve significant advances in energy efficiency, renewable energy, cleaner transit and reduced consumption of natural resources: critical to enabling these advancements is a set of binding agreements to curb greenhouse gases. Despite emerging bipartisan leadership in Washington pushing for action on global warming, the United States has failed to respond to the crisis and in turn has caused further delay of significant and urgent action. Even with a bold new president in the White House in 2009, it will likely take years before US federal action on

global warming is put into effect. Therefore, we need to increasingly act on the state and local level, particularly with the built environment where our local and state leaders have the most influence.

Luckily, there is hope to be found in America's cities: over 600 mayors representing over eighty million Americans have adopted a climate protection agreement. Cities including Chicago, Atlanta and Seattle are embracing renewable energy, energy efficiency and – the topic of this essay – green building. States are leading the way as well with Governors – including Republicans Charlie Crist and Arnold Schwarzenegger – who are bucking the inaction in Washington.

In the midst of the growing action at the local and state level, we must not forget those most vulnerable to climate change – rather we must empower our low-income families to help solve global warming and protect our vulnerable communities from the impact of climate change.

Addressing Poverty and the Environment: Green Affordable Housing

Green building – the practice of increasing the efficiency with which buildings use resources –reduces negative impacts on the environment and human health. But if green building strategies and practices are to become the norm rather than the exception, they cannot be restricted to the province of high-priced 'specialty' designers and builders. Fortunately, the notion of creating architecture that is eco-friendly and affordable is rapidly evolving from the germinal idea of a handful of pioneering and visionary designers (several of whom are profiled in this book) into a thriving architectural revolution that is being realised today in communities around the world.

When I first volunteered with Habitat for Humanity in 1991, the concept of 'green affordable housing' was considered exotic at best. A couple of years later, when I was Chair of Habitat's 'green team' committee – a committee of one – for the Jimmy Carter Work Project that was coming to Los Angeles, my colleagues indulged me and entertained the notion of healthier, energy-efficient affordable housing. At every turn, however, I was thwarted by the architectural committee being unwilling or unable to adapt their designs to maximise passive solar strategies, the materials committee already having their donated products, and so on. The impasse was emblematic of the larger challenges sustainable design had faced in the larger design world up to that time.

When I first started Global Green's green affordable housing initiative in 1995, sustainable building practices were perceived either as luxuries for the virtuous and wealthy few, or else as a pilot 'experiment on the poor'. While a number of designers and builders were starting to embrace resource-efficient green building practices – precious few of their efforts focused on affordable housing, schools, businesses, or any replicable models for urban communities. Green building was generally accessible only to large businesses or affluent homeowners.

Fortunately, in the intervening years, governments, businesses and individuals have increasingly come to acknowledge and respond to the severe threat of human-made global warming. It is now more broadly understood that the construction and maintenance of buildings accounts for much of the world's energy use, for a major portion of overall resource use, and is a major contributor to climate change. Green building, then, is not the noble pipe dream of fanciful idealists; it is a fundamental and necessary strategy to face the urgent challenge of curbing excessive consumption and the acceleration of global warming threatening humanity's future.

However, we also see that solving global warming and addressing poverty through the built environment must also inspire greatness: the everyday must also include beautiful, thoughtful forms that help make our citizens proud of their homes and their community.

Everyday Efficiency

The collection of ecological architecture showcased in this chapter recasts traditional paradigms of everyday and provocative building strategies. Typically, the term 'everyday' implies commonplace and ordinary, close cousins of drab and mundane. On the other end of the semantic spectrum, to be provocative is to be challenging and stimulating, but the adjective often carries further connotations of being impractical, quixotic, even outrageous.

Buildings with everyday applications – homes, schools, offices, etc. – until quite recently tended to be imagined and constructed as bland, characterless boxes; functional, therefore uninspired and literally lifeless. Even worse, schools were built in the 1960s and 1970s to approximate prisons rather than inspiring learning environments. 'Provocative' and dynamic architecture, on the other hand, was mostly confined to lavish, extravagant structures like cathedrals, palaces, monuments, skyscrapers, and museums.

Today's ecological architecture intelligently integrates buildings into the surrounding landscape and reframes outdated dichotomies of everyday/provocative, familiar/unfamiliar, and sophisticated/unsophisticated. Vast improvements in resource efficiency are being achieved today through means that, while perhaps still comparatively unfamiliar to the layperson, need not be confined to exotic or avant-garde architectural categories.

The state-of-the-art in energy efficiency, for instance, goes far beyond installing light bulbs and energy-saving appliances, important and laudable as such measures certainly are. The designs showcased in this chapter use a variety of innovative strategies and approaches: some 'high-tech' and 'futuristic', and others requiring little more than appropriate and deliberate ecological planning. Buildings are oriented to maximise natural lighting and ventilation; tankless water heaters provide hot water on demand; wind scoops capture cooling breezes; strong insulation works prevent heat escape; temperature and lighting are controlled by automated sensors; power is generated on-site through photovoltaic solar panels, wind turbines and geothermal heat from the ground.

Similarly, while water-efficient fixtures like low-flow toilets dramatically lessen water use, the designs in these pages illustrate how water can actually be recycled through the use of water-capturing cisterns that harvest rainwater and storm runoff for washing and gardening. The use of computerised instruments (like smart sprinklers that detect humidity and rainfall levels) is not the only way to cultivate more water-efficient landscapes; simply choosing native plants reduces the use of water, as native wildflowers, shrubs and grasses are less water intensive, especially in arid climates.

The efficient use of non-renewable resources in our buildings reduces more than just waste, carbon emissions, and the impact on our ecosystems; it reduces the financial demand on owners and occupiers by lowering operating costs. As the direct and indirect price of fossil fuels continues to rise, the provocative design innovations highlighted in this book will increasingly become the everyday norm, as these solutions pay for themselves over an ever-shrinking timeframe. Indeed, some high-performance buildings now produce a surplus of energy that can be sold back to the power grid. And since the coal and nuclear plants that currently power much of our grid convert only about one-third of their energy into electricity (with the other two-thirds lost as waste heat), it is becoming ever more economical and responsible to generate as much clean power as possible at the point of use.

Distributed clean, micro, smart grids from renewable sources powering efficient healthy buildings with time-of-use meters — ideally combined with real-time pricing allowing users to reduce energy use when power costs the most, during peak demand periods, and intelligent performance-monitoring systems that send signals not to just building engineers and metre readers, but to the occupants and homeowners. That is a vision we can see helping us combat climate change, and creating better buildings and homes in which we spend most of our waking and sleeping moments.

Our Future - Green Schools

Everyday ecological and economic efficiency in architecture can be realised not only in our homes and offices, but also in schools. How schools are built has a tremendous impact on regional environmental quality, as well as students' performance, the working environment for teachers and staff, and the operating and maintenance costs for school districts. High-performance schools designed with attention to environmental factors such as proper ventilation, material selection, site planning, and adequate daylighting can expect improved student performance, health and attendance.

Over the life of a building, costs related to operations are more than three times higher than the initial construction cost. The potential small increase in construction costs for a green school is paid back multiple times over the life of the building. Additionally, as more high-performance schools are built, design and construction costs will decrease while energy and water savings will increase. Energy consumption in schools can be reduced by employing many of the smart practices found in green homes: energy-efficient lamps and fixtures with occupancy and daylight sensors, using trees to shade buildings to reduce demand for air conditioning, natural ventilation, using programmable thermostats to eliminate the need to shut off heating and cooling systems in a room when there are no occupants, etc.

Green schools reduce water consumption by using efficient technology and fixtures both inside and outside the school building, including low-flow or waterless toilets, automatic shut-off controls for the taps in the toilets, low-flow showerheads in locker rooms, and high-efficiency dishwashers in school cafeterias. To reduce water for landscaping, green schools include native and drought-tolerant landscaping. When irrigation is needed, it is critical to use high-efficiency irrigation systems and use reclaimed water or captured rainwater as much as possible. Basic efficiency measures can reduce a school's water use by at least 30per cent.

Green schools improve the health and consequently the attendance of students. Daylighting is a central component of high-performance design. Providing natural daylight does more than just reduce the need for artificial light, thereby reducing energy costs; it provides biological stimulation for hormones that regulate body systems and moods. Poor indoor air quality contributes to respiratory infections and can trigger asthma attacks, which leads to absences. Finally, green schools provide a unique educational opportunity. When efficient technology and design in new schools are made visible, buildings can become teaching tools and important features of science, math, and environmental curricula.

Smart Cities

Sustainable architecture considers the placement of buildings not only in relation to the landscape, but also in correlation to other buildings. While a 'green building' may stereotypically conjure images of a structure that is off the grid and secluded in nature, such isolated placement has its own detrimental effects on the environment over time. Rustic or 'backwoods' building placement can function as an inadvertent frontline of suburban sprawl, requiring new infrastructure to continually be built outside of a city's expanding borders. Moreover, building in remote areas considerably increases the energy consumption required for transport, raising emissions of global warming-inducing greenhouse gases.

Recognising the accelerating global trend of urbanisation, the smart growth and sustainable urbanism movements champion light urban development, restored and revitalised city centres, high-density/low-impact building, and mixed-use developments that encourage walking, cycling and mass transit. These community-affirming approaches emphasise and enhance what are generally considered the three main components of sustainability: social equity, economy, and environment.

At Global Green USA, our Climate Solutions for Communities initiative is predicated on the interdependence of these three components. A sustainable living environment cannot flourish at the cost of worsened social inequities or economic havoc. Indeed, the challenge of global warming cannot realistically be met without also addressing the issue of poverty. In all of our work providing technical assistance, policy expertise and education, Global Green advances smart solutions to global warming that empower our most disenfranchised citizens to be part of solving global warming, and to benefit directly. Our current work in the ravaged Ninth

Ward of New Orleans — including the project we are developing as the result of our sustainable design competition with jury chair Brad Pitt — embodies these principles.

The devastation wrought on New Orleans by Hurricane Katrina provided frightening testimony that coastal urban and minority communities are at gravest risk from the impacts of global warming. It also showed the realities of climate change are here and growing. To adapt to the current realities and prevent the worsening of global warming that put hundreds of millions of citizens at risk, we must make efficiency the everyday.

Action, Action, Action

Friedrich von Borries in conversation with Klaus Töpfer

Friedrich von Borries co-manages the Berlin-based architectural office raumtaktik-spatial reconnaissance and intervention together with Matthias Böttger.

Klaus Töpfer is the former Under Secretary General of the United Nations and Executive Director of the United Nations Environment Programme (UNEP).

FvB For many years, you have been a leader of important institutions that are linked to architecture and sustainability. You have been *Federal Minister of Environment, Nature Conservation and Nuclear Energy* and *Federal Minister of Regional Planning, Building and Urban Development* in Germany, and you were Executive Director of United Nations Environmental Programme. In this capacity you have been involved in questions of architecture, urbanism, development and sustainability. Against this great personal and professional background I would like to ask you: What are the most important topics that we have to work on?

KT Let me start with a personal experience I had just a few months ago. I had just spent some days in our small house in Turkey on the Aegean Sea, next to the Greek islands, opposite the lovely island of Lesbos and directly on the beach. As always, we took some trips with a little boat, swimming between the beautiful and picturesque islands. Then, on the second last day of our holiday, an unexpected event destroyed this idyll. Coming back from one of our boat trips, some fishermen in the harbour of our little village told us that they had found eight Africans out at sea, all dead. Those eight Africans did not reach the newspapers or the television news. It seems that this is already a normality. These events touch our everyday lives only coincidentally and when they do, it is shocking. It is only when we are confronted personally that we become aware of what is happening. Thus, if we talk about sustainability and humanity, we have to keep in mind what is happening, every day, on the borders of Europe, even if the news is not reporting these events any more.

As we all know, the Minister of the Interiour of the Members of the European Union has decided to develop a new military police force to protect the outer borders of the European Union. Do we really believe that this is a solution for upcoming global migration? Is that what we mean when we speak about sustainability and humanity? No, it is not.

Global migration and its economic and ecological causes are the most important issues facing us. How will we cope with a world of 8.5 billion people? Right now there are already 6.5 billion. When I was born, seventy years ago, there were only 2.6 billion. Thus, with regard to this demographic development, we are confronted with a new dimension of global migration. We may ask why so many people – like the eight Africans who died near the Turkish coast – are trying to leave their homes and move to another continent? The answer is very simple – look at the world we live in. Here, in the North, we live in wealth; almost everybody can afford housing, cars, food and education. In the southern part of the hemisphere, many people do not have enough food to feed their children. This is an unjust world, an imbalanced world.

As director of the United Nations Environmental Programme (UNEP), I lived in Africa for more than eight years. And I saw that if we cannot reduce these imbalances, we will have to construct new walls. We will have to transform Europe into a fortress. We will be able to do wonderful things within this fortress, but I do not believe that it will be a stable world. Overcoming global imbalance will be the challenge for our children, but we have to start on this challenge now.

FvB How can we act against growing injustice; how can we fight the growing gap between the wealthy North and the suffering South?

KT What is now happening on a global level is what I once called the developed world's ecological aggression against the developing world. I would like to give an example: over the last sixty years, we have increased fishing from the oceans forty times. And while we complain that people from the poorer countries who are trying to come to Europe to share our wellbeing, we are sending our fishing fleets to harvest the fish on their coasts – because we have already overfished the resources along our own coasts. Over that same period, we have also tried to explain why it is a good idea to subsidise our agricultural industry, subsidies that destroy the possibilities of agricultural growth in developing countries. This is neither sustainable, nor is it humanitarian.

In order to fight this imbalance, we have to start asking: What is necessary to create a more just world? One prerequisite is the fostering of economic development in the poor and poorest countries of the world. But in order to have growth, we need nature, the capital of nature. It is always the capital of nature that is the bottleneck that holds up development in the world and not the capital of finance. Here, the rich countries will have to help the poorer countries. Why are we not immediately starting to reduce the export of the costs of our well being to other parts of the world? Germans export quite a lot of CO2 to other parts of the world. German per capita consumption is something like ten tons per year. The average African is linked to less than half a ton. But they are the people who are suffering most. What we can do is work together with the Africans to realise innovative projects like the solar updraft tower, projects that help produce electricity in a sustainable way. Some of this electricity could even be exported. The solar updraft tower by Schlaich Bergermann Solar shows a promising approach, but it cannot be realised without the support of the German government. In addition to the power plant itself, an infrastructure of grids would be needed in order to export this clean energy. But how is the infrastructure to be built in these countries? Can we subsidise it? Can we reduce the gap that is dividing the world?

As ever, money is the most important argument for not doing this. But this is a great misunderstanding. Environmental policy is distribution policy. Environmental policy never, ever creates costs. The costs are already there. There is only the question of who pays for the costs. Are these integrated into the price that we pay when we consume, are they postponed to a future date? Are they distributed to

other regions in the world or are the costs simply borne by nature itself? And that is exactly what we are doing today. We are postponing our problems to a future date or exporting them to other parts of the world. There was a time when the ecosystem was able to integrate this behaviour. The economic development process of the North was fully subsidised by the earth's atmosphere. Carbon dioxide emissions did not lead to carbon dioxide costs.

Now other countries are coming: China, India, Brazil, South Africa, the countries of the developing world that need development. And they have a right to development. And then we, the wealthy, rich countries of the North, proclaim: we want you to develop, to grow, but friends, watch out for carbon dioxide, the atmosphere is already full of it. After having subsidised our own economic process by zero CO2 costs, we now want the developing countries to pay for this act. The developing countries are not convinced that this is the best way to overcome the gap. And they are right; it would not be a fair deal. Therefore we have to help these countries, and we have to transfer new and sustainable technologies. We have to give the developing countries the proof and the perspective that sustainable development, real sustainable development, makes sense for them.

FvB   Do you believe that this will happen? In many cases, terms like sustainability are used to disguise other interests or just as marketing tools.

KT   Sometimes I am rather sceptical. In all the years since the *Brundtland Report* was published in 1987, sustainable development has changed into a word that is used in an inflationary way. It is almost something that you cannot call into question. There are a lot of situations around the world, where, knowing that the environment and sustainability now sells very well, people tend to try to greenwash their interests. I am always very cautious about this, I have learned to look twice and to look again. We have to go back and ask some very simple questions: in what way is the project contributing to economic development, urgently needed in developing countries for job creation? What is necessary to balance the social structure of the world, knowing that globalisation means a much more differentiated society? What we need is a new attitude. Currently, we are moving apart instead of integrating, resulting in an ongoing and increasing imbalance. We need integration, not further division.

FvB   Can our buildings and our cities contribute to this process of integration? What architecture and cityscapes will we have in future? Will we have to change our concept of architecture and urban space; will we have to develop new design methods?

KT   In his book *Im Gegenlicht*, Joachim Fest wrote a wonderful sentence: 'First we build our buildings and then the buildings build us.' This is very important: we are influenced by our buildings and by the structures of our cities. Architecture is highly underestimated. Do we really believe that the architecture in the banlieus of Paris or in other places in Europe makes no contribution to the conflicts of segregation? Yes, buildings are indeed building us. Cities are building us.

There are already many interesting approaches to a new kind of architecture that makes a contribution to humanity and sustainability. But we have to transform the approaches into actions. By making buildings and projects like the ones presented in this book, for example. This must continue, we all need to go forward. It is not about one star in the sky. We have to multiply all these interesting approaches. We have to bring the shining stars of sustainable and humanitarian architecture down to Earth. There is a need for new architecture, a need for new buildings. An average German person has a per capita square metre of housing of around 42 square metres. An average Chinese person has less than 5 square metres. But

this is going to change, huge investments are being made. These new houses might be constructed in a sustainable way, or they might not. This is a challenge for the future of architecture and engineering. But it is not just about architecture; it is about the whole concept of the city. I do not believe that a world that has to be run with 80 per cent less CO_2 can have the same urban structure as we have now. Who is studying this? Who is making proposals of how to change the city for a world that, in forty-three years time, must run with 80 percent less CO_2? How can we prevent mobility? How can we change not only the mode of traffic, but also the need for traffic? These are important urban issues that we need to find solutions for. We need new ideas for new cities. And instead of words, words, words, we need action, action, action.

Projects

Cape Schanck House

Private Residence
Victoria, Australia
2006

Paul Morgan Architects

Melbourne Victoria, Australia

[1] | South façade
[2] | East deck entrance with view of
neighbouring property

The Cape Schanck House is located near rugged coastline subject to strong prevailing winds and sits within an expanse of native tea trees. The adistinctive pattern of tree growth is caused by light stimulus, or phototropism, and causes the trees to form a natural 'tunnel' at the west of the site. The dynamic forces of wind energy, wind turbulence and phototropism have informed the modelling of the building envelope, bulb tank and columns. The flows through the site inform the linear site nature of the east and west decks that extend into the landscape. The patterning of the pavers was based on the nearby rock platform, where fast-cooling lava forms into sequential patterns of pentagons and hexagons.

The central element of the internal space – the large bulb-shaped tank – contributes to the environmental performance of the house in two ways: it collects and stores rain water harvested from the entire roof surface, while the 6 mm mild steel tank walls keep the water at a temperature close to 21°C, ambiently cooling the house interiour.

Excess water drains to an external tank, and this water is used for flushing toilets, irrigating the garden, washing wetsuits and occasionally for drinking.

On the south elevation, wind scoops amplify cooling southerly breezes during summer by trapping and directing cooling winds into the house, whilst providing shade from the hot afternoon sun.

Early indications are that the success of the water tank's cooling effect, aided by cross-ventilation, is more than could have been hoped for. Together, these environmental measures eliminate the necessity for air conditioning even during the extreme temperatures of Victoria's summers.

The micro and macro environmental context was considered carefully at all stages of the design. The stand of established tea trees on the site was respectfully used as a generative element in the design strategy. The formal envelope and positioning of the house on the site was profoundly influenced by an observation and exploitation of the natural growth patterns produced by the trees' response to sunlight (phototropism) and wind. The tea trees were retained as far as possible in the realisation of the building. In choosing plants for landscaping around the house, species were selected from those that belong to the local ecosystem.

[1]

[2]

[1]

[2]

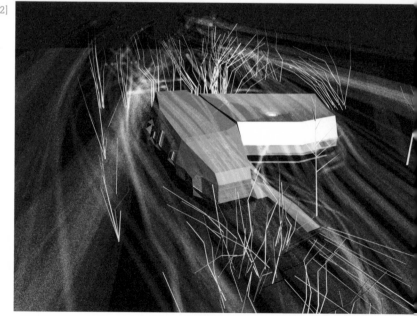

[1] | West elevation of the Cape Schanck
House, which sits within an expanse
of native tea trees.

[2] | The building is subject to strong
prevailing winds. The flows through
the site inform the linear site nature
of the east and west decks that extend
into the landscape.

[3]

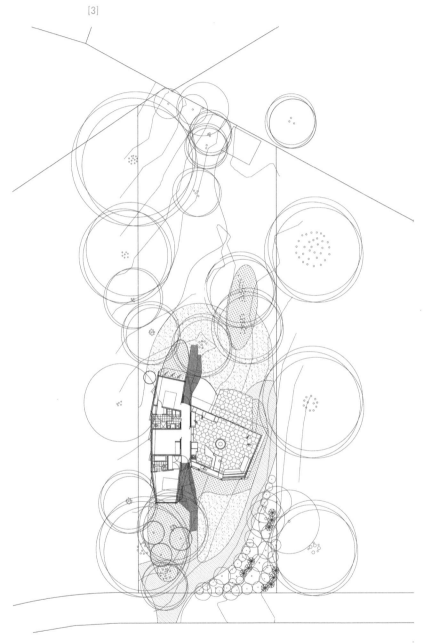

[4]

[5]

[3] | Site plan
[4] | The rugged coastline of the
         surrounding area
[5] | East elevation of entrance view

[1]

[2]

The modelling of the form produced an aerodynamic external skin and continuous internal skin. The wind scoops on the south elevation are a kind of peeling of the outer skin. Turbulence is also inflicted upon the skin. Where the wind modelling showed compression and turbulence around the front entry area, panels are warped as the idea of wind pressure forced into a contained space takes effect. In these instances nothing is added on, rather the skin is disturbed. Vertical louvers on the rear bedroom have a machine-like quality, and yacht technology was employed in the detailing. The 'underskin' flows continuously from the external eaves to the ceiling, and is 'gathered' into the bulb tank.

Nowadays, public debate in Australia is largely about the environment and global warming. Most of the highest temperatures of the past century have occurred in the last ten years. Water catchment capacities have fallen to alarming levels and water restrictions have been applied by the government. In this context, the water tank is the most significant element of the Cape Schanck house. It is the focus of the house, displacing the fireplace and hearth to a secondary role. It organises the living area into four discrete areas: kitchen, living, eating and work. The tank cools the ambient air temperature during summer, stores and supplies rainwater, and structurally carries the roof load.

[1] | East elevation
[2] | North elevation
[3] | Ground floor plan
[4] | Cross-section

[3]

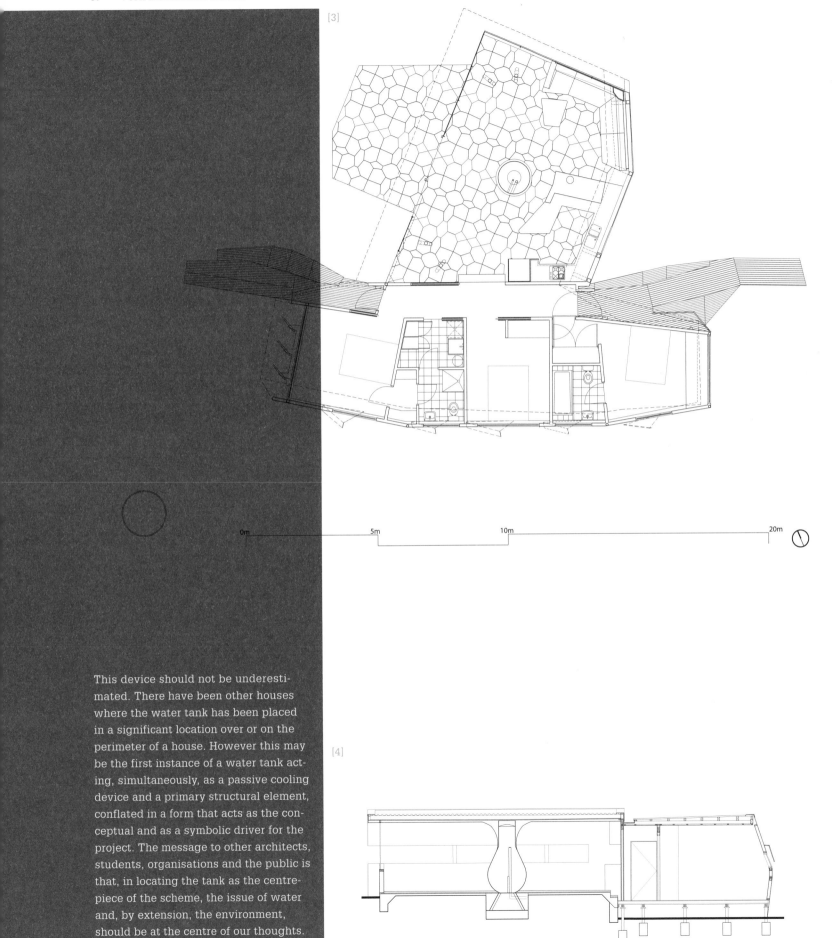

0m   5m   10m   20m

[4]

This device should not be underestimated. There have been other houses where the water tank has been placed in a significant location over or on the perimeter of a house. However this may be the first instance of a water tank acting, simultaneously, as a passive cooling device and a primary structural element, conflated in a form that acts as the conceptual and as a symbolic driver for the project. The message to other architects, students, organisations and the public is that, in locating the tank as the centrepiece of the scheme, the issue of water and, by extension, the environment, should be at the centre of our thoughts.

[1]

[2]

[1] | Interiour view
[2] | The large bulb-shaped tank is the
central element of the house and
contributes to its environmental
performance.

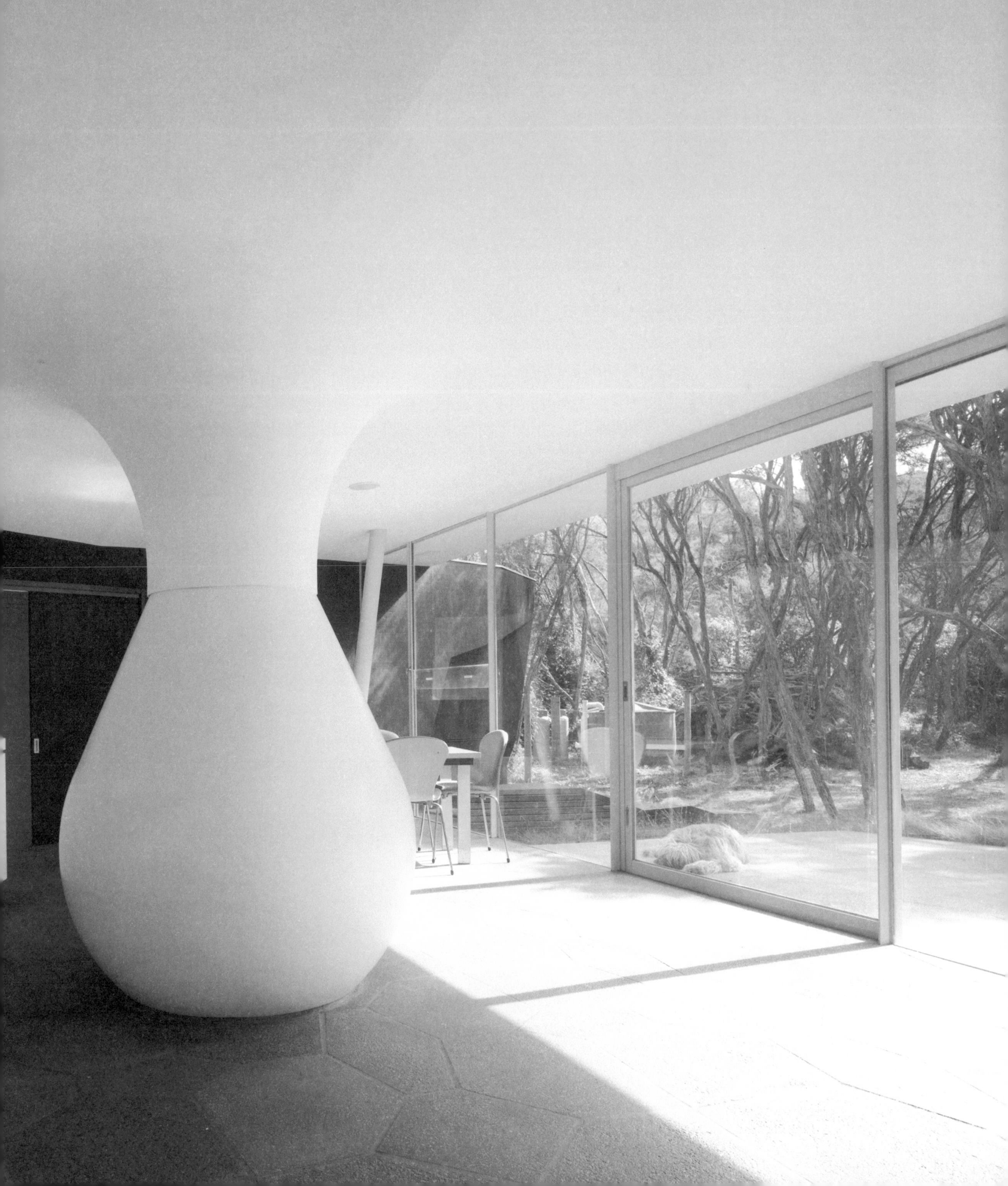

OKO House

Private Residence
Byron Park, London, UK
2006 (ongoing)

Youmeheshe
Architects

London, UK

The OKO House aims to provide an innovative design that makes a carbon neutral, environmentally responsible prefabricated house available to the mass market. The prefabricated form is more about convenience and freedom; with available technology, sustainable bespoke architectural solutions are here offered at the price of mass production or mass customisation.

The design of the house strives towards a constitutionally organic building. Each house 'touches the ground lightly', physically respecting its relationship with the earth. A central core, constructed using engineered timber, forms a structural 'spine': a timber frame that extends from pile foundations to allow two balanced accommodation wings to span out over the landscape.

This project explores what can be achieved within a small house; the layout is clean and rational but can be varied to suit individual living requirements. The interiour can be altered, as families grow larger or smaller, with floors being added to create new bedrooms and removed to create double-height living rooms or even a roof garden.

The central core is a conduit for the services allowing the side wings to be adapted to varying requirements. The core also forms storage, a chimney and, at its base, a biomass fireplace: the heart of the home. The design creates a

new profile thanks to the logic of off-site construction and the volumetric configuration of spaces that allow natural ventilation, maximisation of daylight and the opportunity of reconfiguration.

The design is based on prefabricated or modular components, enabling fabrication of key elements to be carried out in a controlled environment; physically and socially. The result is a house shaped by consistent quality in material, detail and assembly.

The timber structure is produced using off-cuts from the production of soft wood plank doweled together to form large timber panels, solid wood construction. Although the house forms may look complex, the individual timber component shapes are nested within standard-sized timber boards with the aim of minimising waste. Complex abutments between panels can be created using a robotically controlled six-axis cutting machine, enabling the form to move away from the typical perpendicular building products. This construction strategy aims towards a synthesis between CAD and CAM.

Of all building materials, timber consumes the least energy across its lifecycle; wood structures are carbon negative. A combination of a super-insulated structure, a heat exchanger and the orientation of the building means that all heating energy required can be obtained from passive solar gain through the

large triple-glazed façades and the mobilisation of ground source heat. Thanks to passive heating, the house receives constantly filtered fresh air, creating a clean and healthy internal environment.

Water collected from the roof is piped to a storage unit located within the cladding zone, adding further thermal mass. Grey water can be stored above the toilet area allowing a gravity fall system to supply the toilets.

[1] | OKO House single building unit
[2] | Exploded view of the modular
       components
[3] | Interiour view
[4] | Master plan for Byron Park,
       London, UK

[1]

[2]

[3]

[4]

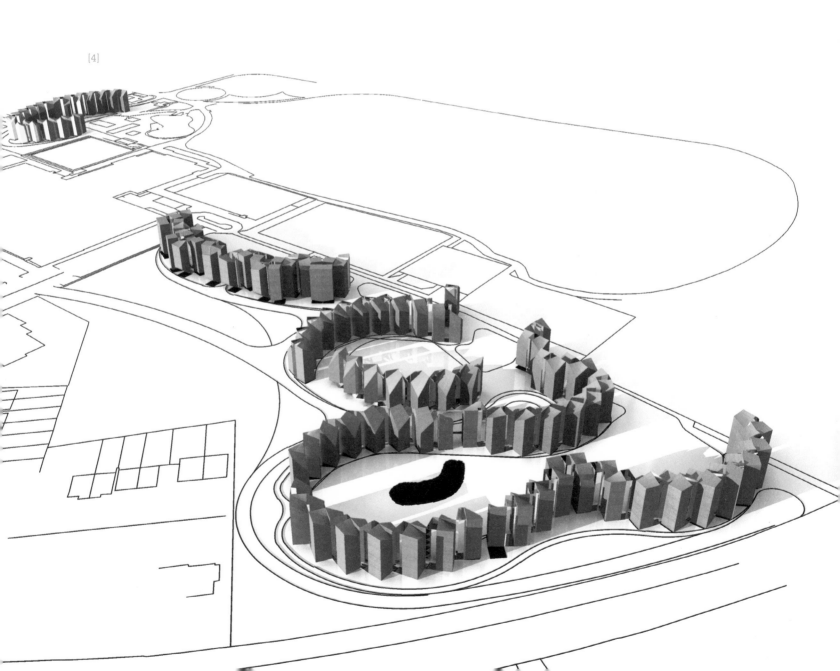

H16

Private Residence
Stuttgart, Germany
2006

Werner Sobek

Stuttgart, Germany

Werner Sobek advanced the design concept, originally developed for his own house, the famous R128, for the private residence, south of Stuttgart: a maximum of transparency and a minimum of structure, full recyclability, extremely high user-comfort through integrated building automation and very flexible ground plans, and – last but not least – zero emissions thanks to intelligent climate engineering and highly efficient building materials. In addition, particular attention was paid to the integration of the building into the surrounding landscape, allowing for magnificent views over the town and the valley lying below. Seen from afar, the house blends harmoniously into nature.

The H 16 house consists of two contrasting cubes responding to the particular situation on an inclined plot. The transparent, all-glass cube features an open living space with a flexible ground plan and the greatest possible transparency. The black cube accommodates the private rooms, thus ensuring intimacy and quiet spaces for retreat. A natural stone wall provides the slope with an enclosed space and frees up space for the cubes.

The ensemble is augmented by a light-coloured cube, which is visually connected to the residential building by a steel terrace. This cube houses the garage and building services. All three cubes have a supporting structure of steel that can be built up (and dismantled) within a couple of days. The steel structure is fully recyclable, as are all other materials in the house.

The transparent cube sits on top of the black cube, protruding on one side by more than six metres. It has highly insulating triple glazing, which not only facilitates a pleasant room climate, but also allows full transparency and beautiful panoramic views of the surrounding landscape. The large glass panes can be opened on three sides as sliding doors. The glass has a special sun protection coating. Additional protection is offered by textile glare shields that can be moved up and down at the push of a button.

The open living space in a highly
insulated triple-glazed cube. Large
glass panes can be opened on three
sides as sliding doors

[1]

[2]

[1] | View of the connecting staircase and
       the town and valley lying below.
[2] | South elevation. Despite its cubic
       forms, the house seen from afar blends
       harmoniously into the surrounding
       nature.

[1]

[1] | North-west elevation. A natural
       stone wall provides the slope with an
       enclosed space and frees up space for
       the cubes.
[2] | South elevation

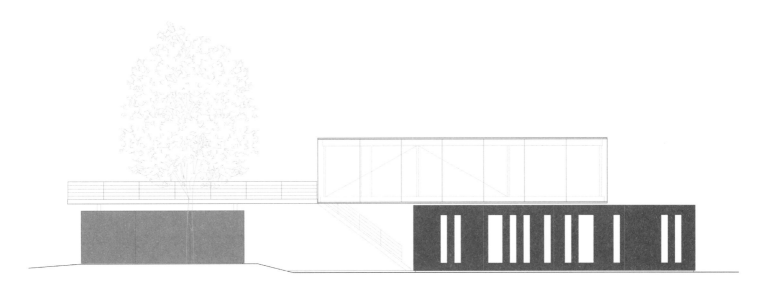

[2]

The black cube is constructed from prefabricated architectural concrete sections. The surface of these concrete sections was finished by a stonemason to give it an amorphous character and great tactile quality. Ceiling-high (but very narrow) windows provide generous lighting and exciting views – without disturbing the very private character of these rooms.

The two cubes are connected by a fanfold flight of stairs made of stainless steel. The stairs are flanked by a red cabinet that links the two cubes to each other equally. The cabinet covers the full height of the black cube and goes up to parapet height in the transparent cube.

A specially adapted climate concept allows for emission-free heating and cooling. The utilisation of ground heat (geothermal heating), in connection with a heat-pump system, mechanical prime ventilation and a photovoltaic system ensures that the edifice can function without fossil fuels altogether: in energy terms, the building is entirely self-sufficient. Thus it is fully sustainable, not only with regard to its building materials and its structure, but also to its energy system.

Temperature is easily regulated at the push of a button via a touch screen or by remote control: the same applies to turning lighting on and off, the opening and closing of doors and windows, etc. The automation of the building makes an important contribution to the very high level of comfort achieved throughout the house.

The H16 house is a tribute and, at the same time, an equal, to outstanding icons of modern architecture.

The building combines sustainability (zero emissions and full recyclability), state-of-the-art design and first-class building technologies, thus making it an achievement from an architectural, technical, and aesthetic point of view.

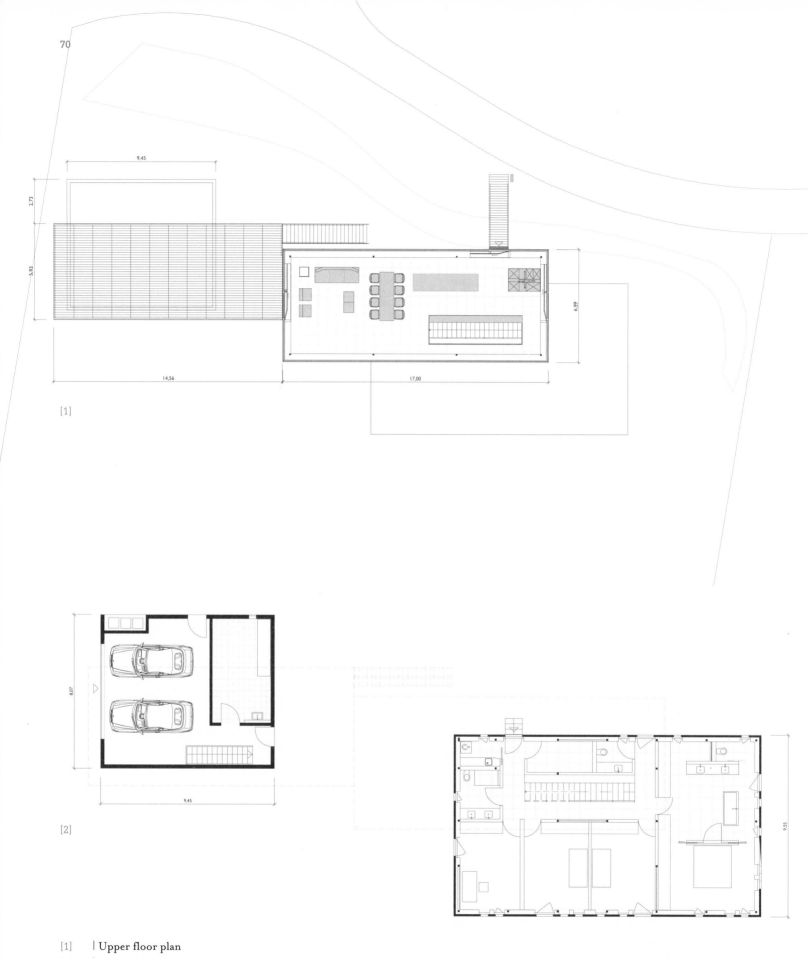

[1]

[2]

[1] | Upper floor plan
[2] | Ground floor plan
[3] | North-east elevation

[3]

Lufthansa
Aviation Center

Office Building
Frankfurt a.M., Germany
2006

Ingenhoven
Architekten

Düsseldorf, Germany

The new Lufthansa headquarters are at the centre of Europe's most efficient transport junction where Frankfurt Airport, motorways, and ICE high-speed train lines intersect. The comb-like building plan of the Lufthansa Aviation Center (LAC) has ten wings and encloses landscaped gardens that act as buffer zones, insulating the building against air-pollution emissions and noise.

Plants chosen from five continents symbolise Lufthansa's global connections. All 1,850 office workstations have views into the glass-roofed gardens and can be naturally ventilated. The open central passage connects the different areas. On completion of the second stage of construction, this communicative building will house 4,500 employees and include building wings surrounding twenty-eight gardens.

The roof of the new Lufthansa Aviation Center at Frankfurt Airport is 55,000 square metres of glass lattice inspired by the shape of a paraglider. The futuristic office building provides 1,800 people with a light and airy space in which to work, not only at state-of-the-art workstations, but also in nine indoor gardens. As a certified 'low energy building', the LAC requires only one-third of the energy of a conventional office building.

The building is supposed to reflect Lufthansa's corporate philosophy by combining the aviation group's business policy with ecological considerations and sustainability. Planning states that the heating requirements are 60 per cent below the limits mandated by the German Thermal Protection Ordinance (Wärmeschutzverordnung), putting it on the level of the low-energy household standard. Efficient lighting and enhanced energy and air transport keeps electrical consumption low.

The atria are naturally ventilated and, as 'climate buffers', they play their part in ensuring low heating-energy consumption in the building. In winter, the temperature will not sink below zero degrees Celsius; during the summer, temperatures are that of a moderate Mediterranean climate. The gardens are not just a part of the energy conception; they also have a considerable overarching spatial quality.

74

↘ | The naturally ventilated atria act as 'climate buffers' and ensure the low heating–energy consumption of the building

The barrel-shaped grid shells above the atria are composed of bend-resistant, welded rectangular steel sections; these link the s building sections across a span width of roughly eighteen metres.

The roof component was aerodynamically optimised with the help of experiments in fluid mechanics. Spoilers were added to create a permanent neutral pressure zone above the roof component. Without these spoilers, wind would press down on the roof surfaces and force air back into the atrium. The component can be opened or closed by means of a motorised flap depending on climate conditions. On the façade side, the elements of the thermoactive ceiling system, the electrical conduits and the sprinkler ducts are installed next to the concrete binding beam, as are the external sun and glare-protection elements.

Great openness dominates in this building. Each office faces towards one of the gardens, and is naturally aired and ventilated by the garden.

Open zones support communication and spontaneous interaction. The sustainable flexible structure also means that the typology of the offices allows unlimited adaptability.

[3]

[2]

[1] | Great openness dominates the
        entire building.
[2] | Open zones are designed to support
        communciation and spontaneous
        interaction.
[3] | Entrance lobby

| Entrance elevation. The building is squeezed in between one of the most heavily used German highways, the ICE high-speed railroad line from Frankfurt to Cologne, with the airfield to the south.

↘ | The 55,000 square metre glass
lattice roof is inspired by the shape
of a paraglider.

project

Palestra
Building

Office Building
London, UK
2006

architects

SMC Alsop

London, UK

| Since 2006, the Palestra Building
has been the new home of the
London Development Agency and the
London Climate Change Agency.

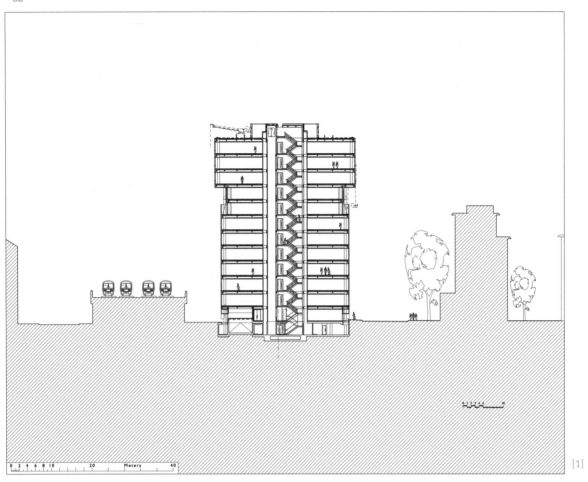

0 2 4 6 8 10   20   Meters   40

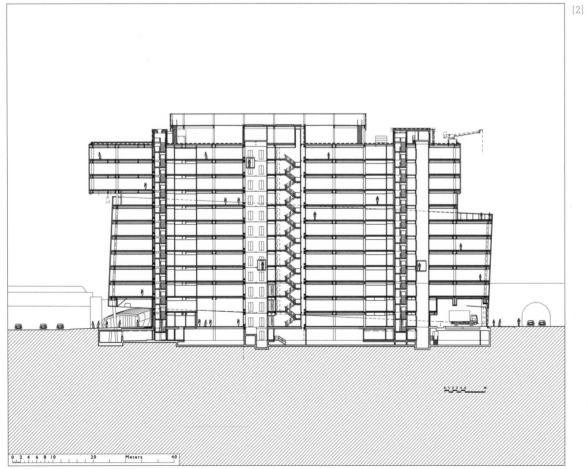

0 2 4 6 8 10   20   Meters   40

As its distinctive form has taken shape over the last years, the Palestra office development, designed by SMC Alsop, has attracted considerable public and professional interest. The completion of Palestra has introduced a significant new addition to both the South London streetscape and the London commercial office market.

The building, in Blackfriars Road directly opposite Southwark Tube Station, has an adventurous design, but is located in a so far underdeveloped area. The relocation of The London Development Agency (LDA) and the London Climate Change Agency (LCCA) in 2006 to the Palestra can thus be understood as London's contribution to the regeneration of the Southwark neighbourhood. As a high-quality designed office building, equipped with state-of-the-art energy-saving technology, the Palestra presents a convincing renewable energy system that combines photovoltaic technology and building-integrated wind turbines, thus exemplifying London's commitment to sustainability.

As a responsive and inclusive, organisation, the LDA is keen to position London as an exemplary sustainable world city. The LCCA was set up by the Mayor of London to help reduce carbon dioxide emissions from the city. It is a commercial company, wholly owned, controlled by and housed in the London Development Agency. The work of the LCCA is also a key part of the Mayor's commitment to making London a sustainable world city. Its objective is to deliver projects that reduce greenhouse gas – mainly carbon dioxide – emissions from London. The goal of the Mayor's Energy Strategy is to reduce emissions in London by 20 per cent by 2010 from a 1990 baseline, being the first step to achieving a 60 per cent reduction by 2050.

Prior to their relocation, the LDA and LCCA announced the installation of a combined renewable energy system of photovoltaic roof panels and fourteen building-integrated wind turbines. This is the first commercial use of a combined solar and wind power system in the UK. Carpeting and other interiour materials were chosen for their sustainability. The design also includes the potential for the fuel cell technology: these are the first offices in London to incorporate this kind of energy.

[1] | Cross-section
[2] | Longitudinal section

[1]

[2]

[1] | The building is located directly opposite the new Southwark underground station in South London.

[2] | The tilted ground-scraping base slab lifts up towards the west, cantilevering six metres above the pavement to create a dynamic building entrance and public space.

CH2 Melbourne
City Council
House

Federal Building
Melbourne, Australia
2006

DesignInc

Melbourne, Australia

The City of Melbourne aims to achieve zero emissions for the municipality by 2020. A major contribution to this strategy is the reduction in energy consumption of commercial buildings by half. The Council House 2 (CH2) was piloted in an effort to provide a working example for the local development market. The brief required a building that relied, as far as possible, on passive energy systems, while also producing a high-class building.

Compared with the City of Melbourne's existing Council House, the CH2 is expected to reduce electricity consumption by 85 per cent, gas emissions by 87 per cent, reduce water mains supply by 72 per cent and produce only 13 per cent of the emissions.

The council house was the first new commercial office building in Australia to meet and exceed the six-star rating system administered by the Green Building Council of Australia. Equally important to its environmental features,

is that it provides 100 per cent fresh air to all occupants with one complete air change every half-hour. The benefits of superior indoor air quality and conservative estimates on energy costs will see the building pay for all its innovation within five to ten years.

The Council engaged additional consultants to achieve the best result through a design process that combined an in-house design and project management team and external consultants and experts in a two-week collaborative design workshop, which resulted in the six-star-rated design solution.

The design achieved this result through a combination of local practices and international innovation including recycled concrete, recycled timber, timber windows, sewer mining and cogenerating using natural gas. Shower towers and phase change material have been employed to produce and store cold water for use by chilled ceilings and beams, while wind turbines are used to extract air during a 'night purge'. Solar hot-water heating and photovoltaic panels take advantage of good solar access as a result of CH2's location within the forty-metre height limit of Melbourne's central business district. The use of mass within CH2's design and construction has allowed the use of the diurnal shift in temperatures in summer to cool the building by opening windows for four hours each night.

↘ | Fresh outside air is drawn in from 17 metres or more above the street and channeled into shower towers, that can be seen on the south façade, and which use use falling droplets of water to cool the air.

The building was designed to be a holistic and all-inclusive system with its occupants as participants. The design follows a model that promotes a more interactive role between city and nature, acting more like an ecosystem in which all parties depend on each other.

With the current concerns about environmental impacts and the health of occupants, CH2 has shown how simple ideas can be used to assist in producing an impressive result. The building's financial viability suggests this kind of building should be the norm. In its procurement, the City made all its information publicly available, including ten independent studies by academics of the various components used in CH2. These studies are placed on the City's website providing complete transparency as regards the building's procurement.

↘ 88 | Vertical gardens run the full height of the northern façade. They assist with shading, glare and air quality.

↘ 89 | North elevation

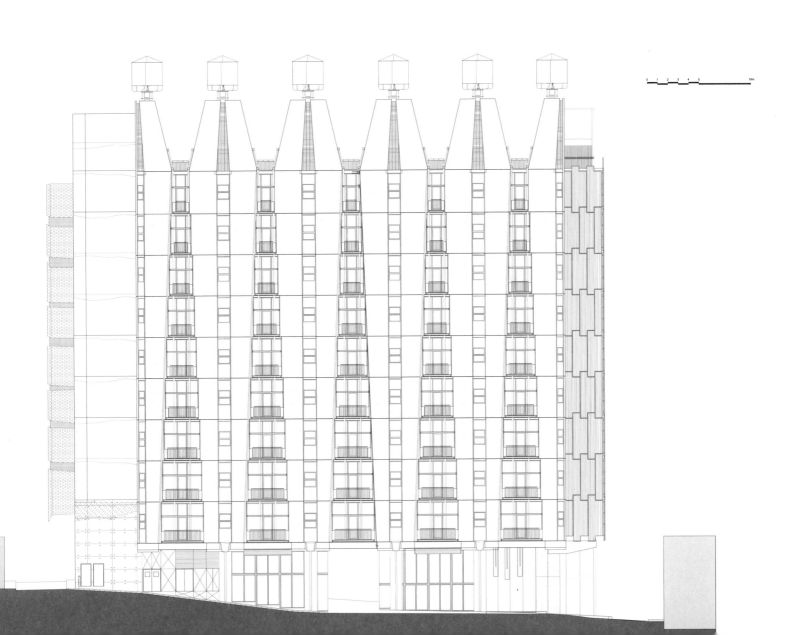

[1]

[2]

↘ 90 | The north façade comprises air extraction ducts that absorb heat from the sun, helping stale air inside rise up and out of the building.

[1] | Louvres made from recycled timber shade the west façade. Energy from photovoltaic panels power the louvres, which move according to the position of the sun.

[2] | Six wind turbines on the roof extract air from the office spaces through ducts on the north façade. The especially designed turbines replace electric fans, that would normally carry out the same function.

Parliament Hill School

School Building
London, UK
2005

Haverstock Associates LLP

London, UK

The building is an extension to the Parliament Hill School in London. It links the existing buildings via a new curved walkway along the south side of the building, providing shelter for students and step-free access across the site. The initial brief set out a need for specialist teaching spaces for the new design and technology department. The building now contains three multimedia labs, a CAD/CAM facility, and ancillary facilities with a non-D&T (design and technology) section for student services. Extensive consultation was carried out to ensure that the final solution was a shared vision between all the stakeholders.

The new sedum roof of the building provides an ecological habitat for the courtyard with minimal requirements for maintenance, and increases the total green area of the school site. The design of the roof aids insulation levels and absorbs surface water run-off so as to regulate and reduce levels of water being fed back into mains sewers. The building runs north-south on the site. The south side has smaller openings with deeper reveals, together with a galvanised steel canopy in order to reduce solar gain in the summer months. The glazing on the north side of the building and the light chimneys maximise natural lighting conditions into the full depth of the lab areas. The light chimneys are cedar clad and form an important landmark within the green roof and allow for stack effect and high-level trickle ventilation.

Internal temperatures in summer and winter are regulated by the use of thermal mass, in the form of exposed pre-cast concrete soffits; together with the external envelope, heat recovery and the heat emitted from occupants, this provides for an almost self-heating building. The hallways are the only spaces directly heated by low temperature radiators; these spaces act as a buffer between the outside and the labs. In the labs themselves, minimal amounts of heat can be transmitted via a heated battery to make up for any shortfalls after heat recovery. When required, initial heat

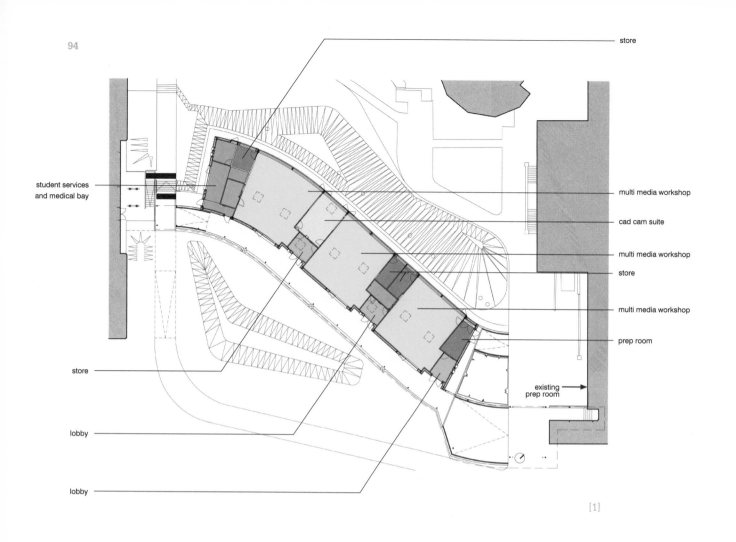

store

multi media workshop

cad cam suite

multi media workshop

store

multi media workshop

prep room

existing
prep room

student services
and medical bay

store

lobby

lobby

[1]

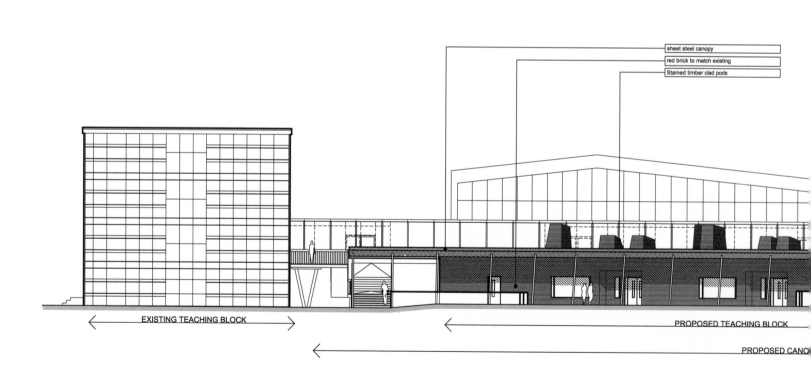

sheet steel canopy

red brick to match existing

Stained timber clad pods

EXISTING TEACHING BLOCK

PROPOSED TEACHING BLOCK

PROPOSED CANO

[2]

source is by means of a high-efficiency domestic-size condensing boiler. Night purging is used in the summer period to reduce overall temperature during day-time operation. High levels of insulation constructed into the external envelope improve on present building regulation targets. Double glazed, argon-filled windows have been used with high-quality thermally broken frames. The passive infrared lighting system, together with linear fluorescent luminaire light fittings, will reduce electrical costs of the building in the long term.

No top soil was removed from site; instead, only excavated material was used to redefine landscape and to provide sculptural grass mounds around the courtyard for students to appropriate. All site rubble was reduced to form hardcore for use in making new paths.

Crushed brick was used for the growing medium on the green roof. Bricks were carefully chosen in order to marry with existing building context and with a view for recyclability at a later stage.

Internally, the building has a robust industrial feel where all services and structure are clearly exposed. Not only does this provide clarity, as regards the process of design by synchronising the essence of the subject area it accommodates, it also ensures, where possible, self-finishing surfaces so as to reduce long-term maintenance requirements. The steel structure is designed with economy of weight and flexibility for the future in mind. As there are no internal columns, walls can be removed at any point and the building can be reconfigured to meet ever-changing educational needs.

[1] | Site plan of the design and technology studios
[2] | South elevation of the design and technology studios

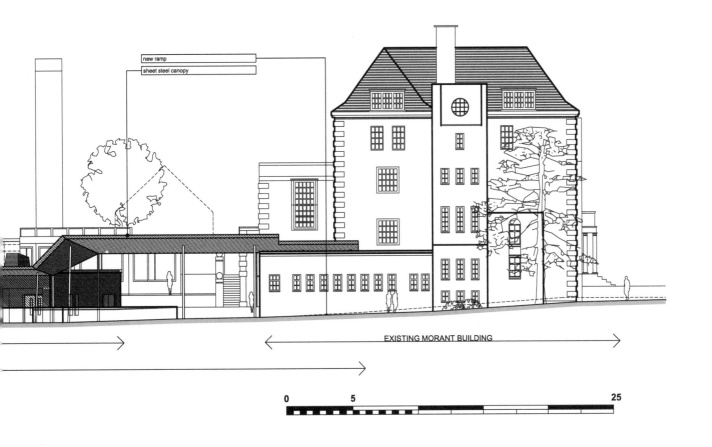

new ramp

sheet steel canopy

EXISTING MORANT BUILDING

0   5   25

[1]

[2]

[1] | Interiour view of the performing
      arts building
[2] | Interiour view of the design and
      technology studios

↘ | North façade with view of heat and
light chimneys

Marie Curie
High School

School Building
Dallgow-Döberitz, Germany
2005

Grüntuch Ernst
Architekten

Berlin, Germany

| Back elevation with outdoor
sport facilities

Schools are key factors for sustainability in architecture, because they shape the next generation's understanding of architecture. A school is the dominant environment in the daily life of students for many years and will form their understanding of the natural and built environment.

The Marie Curie High School in Dallgow-Döberitz connects low-density housing with the open landscape. It is integrated into the landscape to form a new 'urban landscape'. The brief of the architectural competition asked for a 'campus school': a group of small buildings like that of the surrounding housing estate. The final building contrasts this concept with the idea of urban density. The quality of density is the most important factor in the building of suburbia, since nature is the most valuable resource endangered by human settlement.

[1] | Site plan. The two L-shaped wings offer varied sequences of inner-facing and outer-facing sections and open spaces.

[2] | The roof area is a raised deck for use during breaks.

[2] | Entrance situation

[2]

The school is designed like a miniature city with plazas, streets and houses that allow for easy orientation; it has visible units, which help create group identities. Two L-shaped wings offer varied sequences of inner-facing and outer-facing sections and open spaces. The sports hall is sunken and the library, offices and specialist rooms surround a protected school playground. The roof area is a raised deck for use during breaks; it extends above the sports hall and around the central auditorium.

The construction cost is minimised by using modular repetition, even so, the modular repetitions are balanced with contrasting spaces and are linked by surprising visual connections in order to enrich daily life in the building. The floor plans are arranged on the basis of solar-geometric principles. While the classrooms face north, the corridors face south and act as buffer zones. Here the glass façade is prevented from overheating by perforated metal panels, folios and printed layers.

The building is also designed to shrink and expand so that activities can easily move into the outdoor area. The auditorium, for example, is the central main hall. It can be a very closed-off room for some occasions, but it can also be extended into the corridor and linked with the courtyard for other occasions. It can also extend the visual connection onto the upper deck and down into the gym.

The transparent façade maximises natural daylight and reduces artificial lighting costs. Even more importantly: extensive daylight and the feeling of openness calms pupils down and breaks down emotional barriers by enabling them to make visual connections beyond the enclosed space.

The school building is compact and the roofs function as further playgrounds. Therefore the site covers only a minimal surface area. Even though the school is a very firm and deep building, all areas are naturally ventilated: for example, in the gym and auditorium, the openings in the rooflights ensure that a thermo-dynamic breeze moves through this large space.

At night, the building cools down naturally as the ceiling and walls are made from exposed concrete without cladding or suspended ceilings. Thus, these heavyweight structures give up their heat by convention to the cool night air and by radiation to the cold outer atmosphere, thereby recharging their heat-sink capability for the next day. This 'passive night cooling' uses sensors and automatic openings to ensure cross-ventilation.

The connections to the outdoor space provide intense physical experiences for the pupils. This is a positive and confident example of stimulating architecture that is close to nature.

[3]

[1]

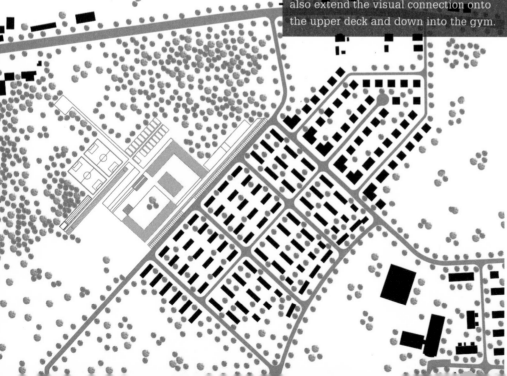

[1]

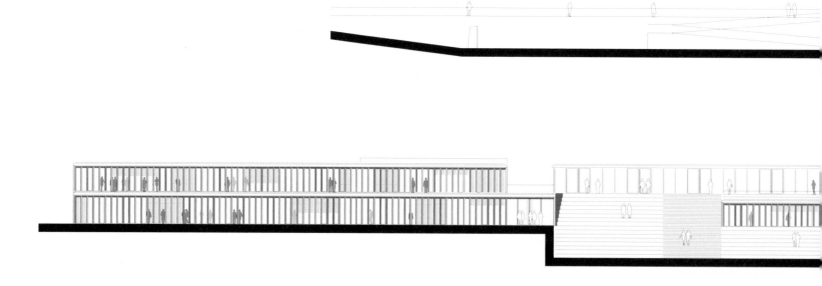

[2]

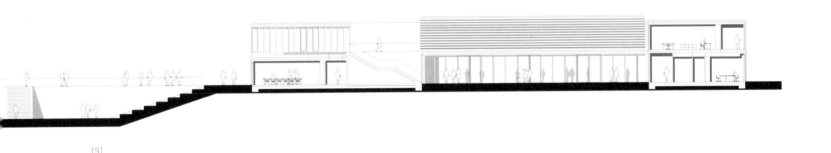

[3]

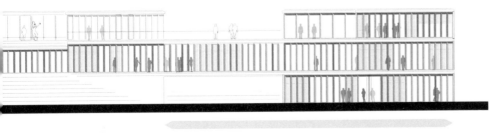

[4]

[1] | Entrance with view of school
        cafeteria

[2] | Entrance with view into sunken gym

[3] | Cross-section

[4] | Longitudinal section

[1]

[1] | Classroom
[2] | Visual connection between upper
      deck and corridors through an
      integrated periscope
[3] | Interiour views. The façade acts as
      a colourful envelope that makes the
      school glow in different ways.

[2]

[3]

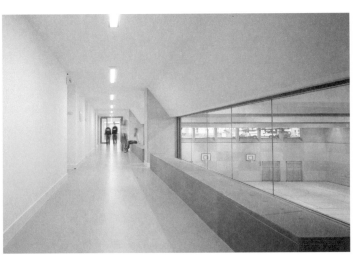

1% Solution

Pro Bono Design Program
2005 (ongoing)

Public
Architecture

San Francisco, USA

Inspired by the examples of the legal and medical professions (such as Legal Aid and Doctors Without Borders), Public Architecture started a new initiative: The 1% Solution.

The 1% Solution programme engages architecture firms to pledge a percentage of their time to voluntary or public interest work. The 1% Solution programme is simultaneously working to educate, attract, and serve non-governmental organisations (NGOs) in need of design assistance. Its efforts to date have focused on the United States, but are receiving increasing inquiries from other countries and plan to expand their effort globally at an appropriate time. Individuals and entities outside of traditional architecture, including disciplines such as graphic design, landscape architecture, product design, etc, are also approaching the 1% Solution programme.

Their objective is to increase and institutionalise both the quantity and quality of pro bono work, in pursuit of a more equitable distribution of professional design expertise throughout all social strata. One of the foremost measuring sticks of 'quality' is the clear incorporation of sustainable/green design principles in all 1% Solution projects. Additionally, and just as important, the protocols will involve the partner receiving design services in order to become educated and to implement new green,

sustainable practices in the delivery of the partner's mission as a result of the 1% Solution process.

Requests for voluntary assistance as well as offers by architecture firms willing to donate their time will be fielded and catalogued through a new, highly-interactive website. The ultimate goals are to create sensible matches, forge productive relationships, and realise outcome-based projects between those in need of assistance and those offering it.

The 1% Solution programme facilitates the volunteerism and goodwill of architects and other design professionals. To date, the involvement of over 140 firms, ranging from sole practitioners to some of the largest firms in the United States has been secured collectively, they have pledged to complete nearly 100,000 volunteer hours on an annual basis. These hours are catalogued via the 1% Solution programme website.

Ecological
Budget UK

Research and Development
Programme
UK
2005 (ongoing)

World Wildlife
Fund UK

Godalming, UK

The Ecological Budget UK is a continuous programme of research and development, which aims to make a contribution to the analysis and modelling of sustainable consumption and production. The project then takes this into practical applications for policy, industry and the built environment.

The programme is run by a partnership, including Stockholm Environment Institute at York, Centre for Urban & Regional Ecology at Manchester, and the WWF-UK.

The Ecological Budget UK is focused on resource flows and ecological footprints, accounting and modelling methods, applications to industry, and applications to policy for the built environment. This programme aims to put technical information side by side with interactive communications. It looks both at what we produce and at what we consume, by going from the regional to the local level and the household level. It shows the measure of real sustainability – for the region, for industrial sectors, for policy options, and for lifestyle choices. It sets a direction for change, which combines economic growth, social welfare and environmental sustainability.
The toolkits are focused on the Resource & Energy Analysis Programme (REAP), a unique modelling system based on the ecological budget methods, with various applications and spin-offs.

REAP is a database and modelling system that calculates the total impact of all kinds of production by industry and consumption by households, at local and regional level. It is now available in Version 1.0, but development on scenario modelling, sectoral applications, appraisal packages and business toolkits is ongoing.

Valley View University

University Building
Accra, Ghana
2005 (ongoing)

Chair for Fundamentals of Ecological Planning and Building

Bauhaus University Weimar
Weimar, Germany

Valley View University (VVU) is the oldest private university in Ghana. Close to the capital Accra, it now hosts around 1,000 people but aims to accommodate 5,000 people on its campus in the future.

In order to create a sustainable campus and to develop, implement and evaluate sustainable methods of urban planning, building, sanitation and agriculture, an interdisciplinary team (Bauhaus University Weimar, University of Hohenheim, Ecological Engineering Society, Berger-Biotechnik and Palutec Company) supported by the German Federal Ministry of Education and Research was formed. New study programmes such as Agriculture, Development and Ecological Engineering

have already been established and further scientific discoveries made during the development period will be integrated into the study programmes.

The Chair for Fundamentals of Ecological Planning and Building at the Bauhaus University in Weimar worked on the ecological master plan and designed several ecological buildings such as the faculty buildings, the university church, the new sanitary block, the guest houses, student hostels as well as the decentralised sanitary systems.

Using the idea of cycle management, the master plan represents an integrated ecological general concept that enables

the optimisation of concepts such as traffic, water and nutrients, open space, energy and waste management. The traffic concept, for example, will concentrate buildings into certain areas, the principle of short distances being used to greatly reduce the length of roads and paths and thus save infrastructure costs, surface area and time. The central campus area is intended to be car-free and will only allow access to service vehicles. The area thus gained is then used for green space such as gardens and farmland. Important ecological design elements such as retention swales and ditches to retain rainwater and nutrient-rich and purified wastewater also help to create liveable spaces and to improve the microclimate in general.

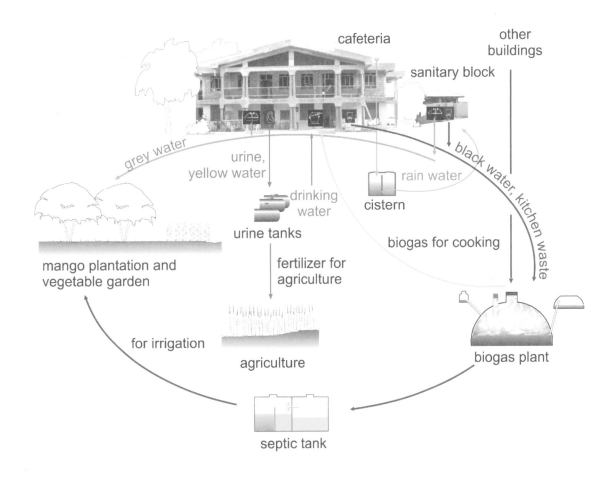

A complex concept of cycles and reuse of wastewater, grey water, urine and organic matter is implemented on the VVU campus and VVU farmland. Within different cells (e.g. building complexes) wastewater is treated differently depending on the amount and composition. A continuous process saves drinking and service water by using appropriate installations (e.g. water-saving toilets and fittings, waterless urinals, etc.). The rainwater collected from the roofs is used for flushing toilets and hand washing. Grey water from various buildings is used to irrigate all kinds of plantations.

The sanitary block near the new cafeteria is as an example of nutrient cycling: it shows the separation of the different substance flows, such as pure urine, urine-water mixture, black water and grey water. All nutrients from urine are used as fertiliser in agriculture. Black water from the sanitary facilities is treated anaerobically in biogas digesters together with organic waste from the kitchen and farms. The collected biogas is used for cooking in the cafeteria. The sludge in the digester can be used as fertiliser in agriculture. The digester outflow is treated in three expansion chambers and then in a septic tank. The purified water is pumped into an elevated tank and used for fertilised irrigation of farmland.

Six department complexes will be built within the central campus area: each department complex will consist of four three-storey buildings, arranged perpendicular to the prevailing wind direction for optimal cross-ventilation. The four buildings are arranged so as to create a large and green central courtyard that can be used during breaks and for open-air lessons. Every complex consists of six lecture theatres, department offices, laboratories, seminar rooms and toilets, which are accessible from the veranda. Overhanging roofs and horizontal and vertical shading devices are used to keep the rooms cool. Because of the low sun, no openings are planned for the north-west and south-east façades.

project

SPREE2011

Waste Water Treatment Project
Berlin, Germany
2007 (ongoing)

architects

Ralf Steeg & LURI.
watersystems

Berlin, Germany

The genesis of the SPREE2011 project lay in the observation of nature: in the interaction between flora and fauna, genera and species in their biospheres.

The River Spree flows right through the city of Berlin – a watercourse through the capital of Germany and a watercourse that has been straightened and polluted.

The river is not polluted by chemical works: the pollution of the Spree has other causes. As in many other cities throughout the world, the sewers in Berlin are designed as a system within which domestic wastewater and rainwater from streets and roofs flow together.

During heavy rainfall, which particularly occurs in summer, the capacity of the sewer network is far exceeded. In this case, the wastewater, although heavily diluted, flows unfiltered into the river. In order to avoid this, it must actually be collected immediately and be placed in intermediate storage before being subsequently transferred to the sewage works. Reinforced concrete reservoirs buried in the ground can deal with this task. However, this method is complicated and therefore very expensive, much too expensive for a local council budget.

SPREE2011 has developed a solution that is considerably more economical than reinforced concrete storage: installing overflow reservoirs made of synthetic

material in the river directly in front of the ducts. After rainfall, wastewater is either pumped back into the sewage system, which now has capacity, or is cleaned on-site.

The design of the overflow reservoirs allows platforms to be created on the water: new urban areas suitable for catering, leisure and service facilities, green areas and swimming pools. Income from rental and utilisation will further contribute to financing the wastewater facilities.

↘ 111 | Beach on SPREE2011 modules

SPREE km 21,190

KIOSK

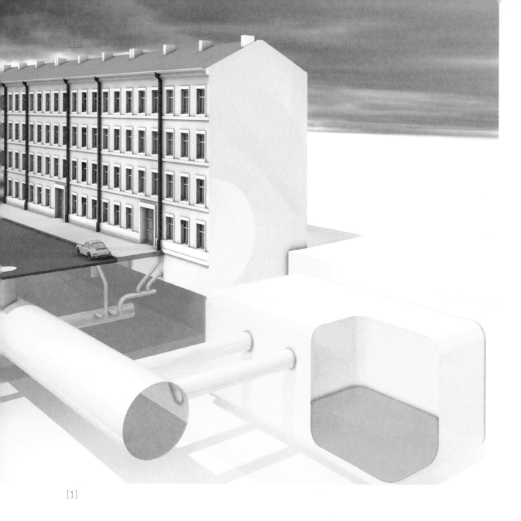

[1]

[2]

This would ideally result in a clean Spree with new islands at the various locations in the centre of the river. Recreation can be transferred from the periphery of the city to its centre, which will be enhanced and a new added value chain will be set in motion. The city will be able to serve as an international example for other cities.

Berlin forms part of the international hydrological cycle; once the city's pollution no longer flows into the Spree and then on to the sea. Hence, a contribution will also be made on a worldwide level.

SPREE2011 is an ecological and economic vision: this sensitive low-tech measure combines ecological, economic, social and cultural aspects.

After five years of preparatory work and several completed studies, the German Federal Ministry for Education and Research made significant subsidies available in April 2007. In collaboration with five consulting engineers and four specialist sections in the Technical University of Berlin, the initiators have set up a pilot facility at Berlin's eastern port.

[1] | Schematic drawing of the SPREE2001 overflow reservoirs that store diluted sewer water.
[2] | Leisure activities on SPREE2011 island.

project

Metro Cable
San Augustin

Public Cable Car System
Caracas, Venezuela
2008 (ongoing)

architects

Urban-Think Tank

Caracas, Venezuela

In 2003, Venezuela's government put forward a scheme to create an infrastructure of roadways in the barrios (neighbourhoods) of Caracas, beginning with San Agustin, (La Vega, Santa Cruz) a community of some 40,000 people, with approximately 573 inhabitants per hectare. The plan would necessitate the destruction of some 300 homes as well as the elimination of the pedestrian pathways and stairs that are the traditional means of navigating the barrio and a central feature of the community's social life.

The first part of the Urban Think Tank (UTT) project involved a new approach to urban planning. A public symposium and presentation, attended by architects, planners, other experts, university activists, and community leaders at the Caracas University was organised to protest against the government plan and to put forth alternatives.

The essential plan components (preservation of a pedestrian-oriented community; mixed-use development; expanded parks, attractive and safe streetscapes; sources of employment) was established by the barrio residents themselves. As a consequence, a cable car system was selected as having the greatest potential for being ideally suited to the terrain, minimally invasive into and minimally destructive of the existing fabric, highly sustainable and flexible. A six-month analysis and planning initiative, undertaken by UTT, enlisted the participation of the Caracas Metro Cable company, a newly founded subsidiary of Metro Caracas, Doppelmayr, the Austrian ropeway manufacturer, climate engineers Transolar and the US civil/structural engineering firm of Silman & Associates.

As a result, government planners abandoned their scheme and adopted the UTT/San Agustin approach. Metro Caracas and Odebrecht Construction formed a design committee and solicited proposals from various architects and planners. The committee awarded the project to UTT and its task force. In April 2007, the project was formally accepted and endorsed as a government priority, when it was inaugurated by the Venezuelan President Hugo Chavez.

| One of the five Metro Cable stations in the Barrio San Augustin

[1]

[1] | Each gondala holds about eight passengers.
[2] | Direction signs for the Metro Cable stations. The cable car system also preserves the pedestrian-based community of the Barrio.

[2]

The system, integrated with Metro Systems of Caracas, is 2.1 km in length and employs gondolas holding eight passengers each; system capacity allows for moving 1,200 people per hour in each direction. There will be five stations, of which two are in the valley and connect directly to the Caracas public transportation system. Three additional stations are located along the mountain ridge, on sites that meet the demands of community access, established pedestrian circulation patterns and suitability for construction with minimal demolition of existing housing. The five stations have a basic set of components and designs in common – platform levels, ramps for access, circulation patterns, materials, and structural elements – but they differ in configuration and additional functions ranging from social, cultural, system administrative functions to gym, supermarket, childcare centre, housing units, public spaces for community gatherings, out-patient healthcare facilities, football pitch and public viewing point.

| Walkways towards the Metro Cable stations. The cable car system's capacity allows for moving up to 1,200 people per hour in each direction.

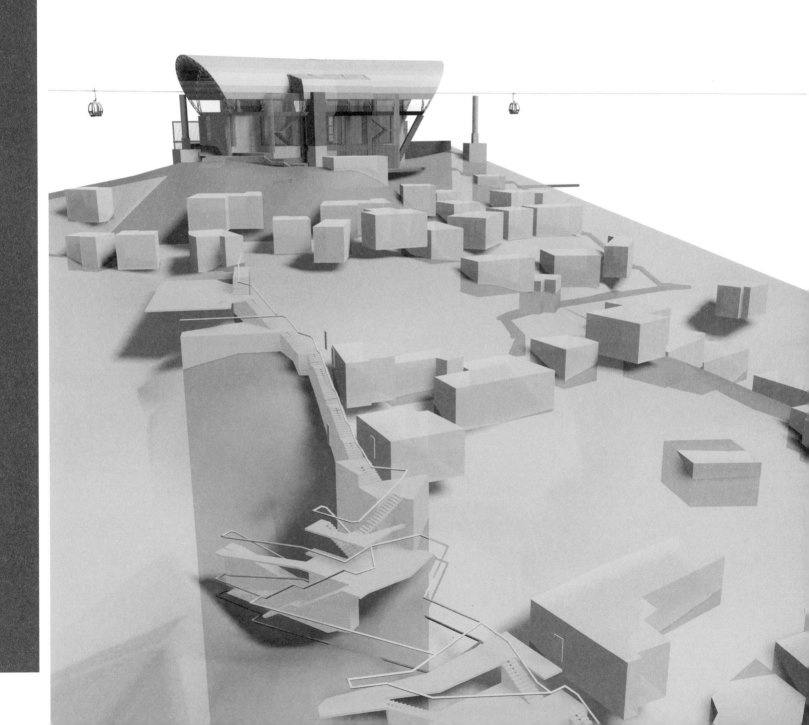

118

118 | Site plan. Two of the five stations are in the valley and connect directly to the Caracas public transportation system.

119 | Despite a basic set up of components and designs, each station differs in configuration and additional functions ranging from social, cultural, administrative, leisure and recreational.

The Caracas MetroCable incorporates a variety of sustainable principles. The materials – primarily steel and concrete – are durable and require little, if any, maintenance and repair. While the cable system itself will draw power from the municipal source, each of the five stations is energy-independent. In the short term, a single wind-driven turbine will provide sufficient power for each station's needs. In the longer term, the shell of the stations is designed to accommodate solar panels, which will eventually provide sufficient power for the energy needs of the entire barrio. The stations and adjacent structures require no mechanical air-conditioning and heating of any kind. Each station

incorporates a 'wind catcher', to direct the prevailing breezes into the interiour. Louvered walls enable fresh air to enter and ventilate the stations. Groundwater will be used for the two valley stations. At the mountain stations, cisterns will hold rainwater for toilets and/or irrigation of residents' kitchen gardens. During daylight hours, the interiors will rely entirely on natural light, brought into the stations both from the sides and through the translucent portions of the shell. After dark, the stations will be lighted with LED lights, as will the public streetscape. The lighting design for the stations contemplates their function as beacons for the community – glowing lanterns that convey welcome and safety.

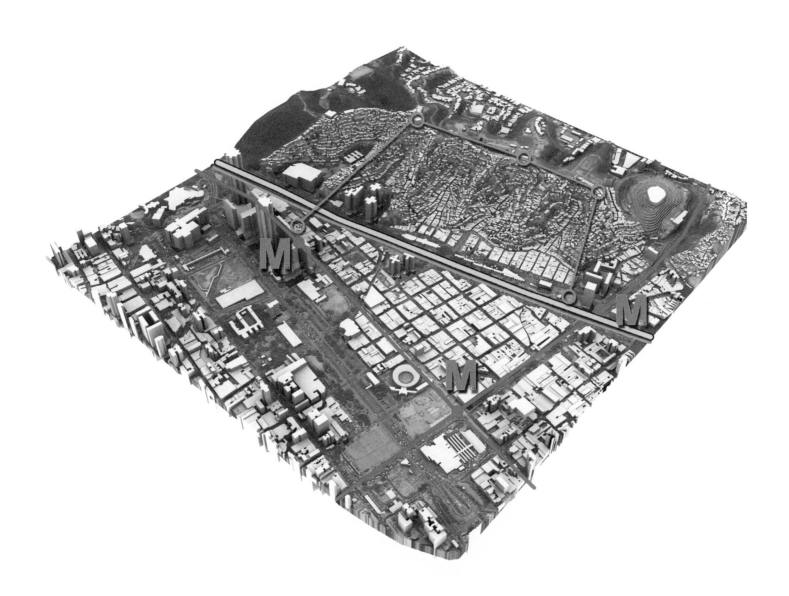

project

Ecoboulevard

Urban Air Trees
Madrid, Spain
2006

architects

Ecosistema Urbano

Madrid, Spain

Ecoboulevard consists of 'air trees' along a new road in a suburban development area of Madrid. The 'air trees' are self-sufficient structures by consuming only that which can produce through its photovoltaic solar energy system.

The proposal for the Ecoboulevard of Vallecas, a suburban extension of the Spanish capital Madrid, can be defined as an operation of urban recycling that consists of the following actions: the installation of three social revitalising 'air trees' placed along the existing suburban area, the densification of trees within their existing concourse, the reduction and asymmetric disposition of the traffic routes, and superficial interventions within the existing suburban area (perforations, backfill, paint, etc.) that result in the reconfiguration of the new built urban development.

Three pavilions, so-called 'air trees', function like open structures to multiply resident-selected activities. Installed in the non-city as temporary prostheses, they will be used only until air-conditioned spaces are no longer needed, when the area becomes 'fixed'. When a sufficient amount of time has passed, these devices are intended to be dismantled; the remaining spaces will resemble forest clearings. Vallecas had

all the negative characteristics typical of suburban developments. Therefore, the Ecoboulevard has been conceived with two objectives: one of a social nature, to generate activity, and one of an environmental nature, the bioclimatic adaptation of an outdoor space.

The 'air tree' is a light structure that is self-sufficient in terms of energy and can be dismantled. It is energy independent, consuming only that which it produces through photovoltaic solar energy collection systems. Selling this energy to the power network will generate a surplus on the annual balance sheet. This will be reinvested into the maintenance of the structure itself. This is just one model for the management of resources on a project over a period of time.

[1]

[2]

[1] | The park area of an 'air tree'
[2] | The pavilions of air trees function
     like open structures to multiply
     resident-selected activities.
[3] | Ceiling view from inside the air tree

[3]

The use of technology plays a critical and decisive role in this project, as it adapts to a real, specific context. The architectural potential of technology lies in its reprogramming and combination with other elements, so that true architectural 'ready-mades' are created. In this case, climatic adaptation techniques, normally employed in the farming sector, have been borrowed.

The autonomy enjoyed by the air trees means that they are exportable objects: they may be reinstalled in similar locations or in other types of situations requiring an urban activity regeneration process (new suburban developments, rundown parks, squares).

The goal of this project is to create an atmosphere that invites and promotes activity in an urban public space that is 'sick' due to 'bad planning'. The simple climatic adaptation systems installed in the air trees are of the evapotranspirative type, often used in greenhouses. This aerotechnical practice – or artificial adaptation – is not a part of a commercial strategy. On the contrary, it tries to undo the link between leisure and consumption and to reactivate the public space through the creation of climatically adapted environments (8ºC to 10ºC cooler than the rest of the street in summer), where citizens can become active participants in public spaces once more.

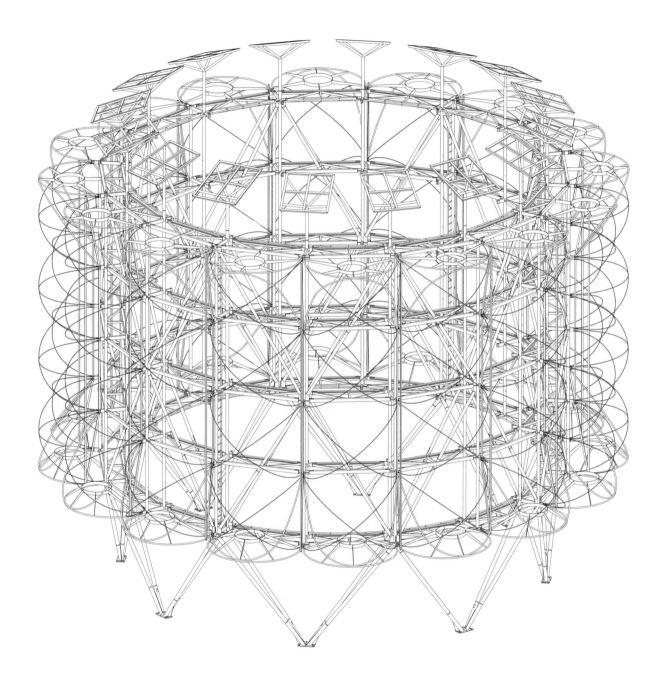

| Technical drawing. The 'air trees'
are objects of an exportable nature.
They can be re-installed in different
locations.

| The air trees are installed in the non-city as temporary prostheses, that will be used only until the inactivity and climatic adaptation problem is corrected.

02

Aesthetics
of
Performance

This chapter illustrates the creative richness of contemporary architecture whose appearance is shaped by ideas on ecological performance. Indeed, it almost seems that the ecological performance of buildings is becoming the new architectural aesthetic. So sustainability is acquiring a new aesthetic dimension in contemporary architecture beyond its pragmatic and ethical relevance.

The Aesthetics of Sustainability

by Leon van Schaik

Leon van Schaik is Innovation Professor
of Architecture at the Royal Melbourne
Institute of Technology (RMIT), Australia.

We all, I think, feel that we understand the ethics of sustainability. Some of us couch these in the terms of our survival as a species on this planet; others in terms of the survival of life on the planet; and others on concepts of fairness: of fair shares of the resources that sustain life. Even if we do not consciously register an ethical position, an ethicist or a critic can examine our practice and describe an ethical position underlying it — one that we may dispute, but while we may rebut the critique we will be unable to dispute that we have an ethical position. Conscious dispute is itself the medium of ethical discourse.

Over the centuries we have developed some principles that govern this discourse. Since Kant, we have been aware that when we claim some 'good' for ourselves, we must consider this claim in the light of what it would mean if all living beings could claim this 'good' for themselves at the same time. Definitions of life expand as our understandings of the universe grow. For sustainability, we need perhaps go no further, but the discourse does have more to offer, and for some reason we have been blind to Kant's principle of 'universalisability'. Since the Nuremberg trials we have argued that those whom we would seek to 'manipulate' for the larger good may only be so 'manipulated' with their informed consent. Today the Australian ethicist Peter Singer argues that this applies to animals as much as to humans. Since the detonation of the nuclear bomb, we have agreed that an ethical position cannot be a statement of abstract principle, but must be formulated with regard to the specific project that we are working on — and on its real and potential outcomes. More recently, our growing understanding of systems of organisation (whether in machines or in living organisms) has given rise to the principle of 'generosity': the principle that the positions that we adopt should open up options for future action rather than shut them down.[1] These nesting principles build upon each other, or contain each other like Russian dolls, or are related to each other as in Gadamer's 'onion': an analogy for the way our understanding grows layer upon layer, always containing and never discarding our former understandings.

Ethical discourse is alive and well. We cannot say the same for aesthetics. Since the excesses of the nineteenth century, aesthetes who admired the sinuous 'line of beauty', preferred the colours cream and green above all others, dressed in velvet, carried a book of poems in one hand, spoke in carefully crafted epigrams and walked around smelling a lily — in control of all their senses — aesthetics have not much concerned architects and their critics. Futurists sought the aesthetics of speed: cars and buildings and even the stationary domestic refrigerator came to be 'streamlined'. Modernism, in particular, spurned the overt pursuit of an aesthetic, arguing for the inevitable 'rightness' of forms determined by function — and failing to account for the prevailing preference for white planarity. Twenty years ago conservatives sought to use aesthetics to support a rejection of all architecture other than the neo-classical,[2] a position that Aldo Rossi had previously espoused on the same basis of a supposed innate popular understanding of the forms derived from ancient Greece and the Roman Empire, but on a more radical social foundation.

Mies van der Rohe's famous dictum 'less is more' is possibly the most quoted aesthetic proposition of late twentieth-century architecture; it is the basic argument underlying minimalism in architecture. On the face of it, it could be taken for an argument that could be used in a discourse on sustainability, like the 'principle of parsimony' in rhetoric that stems from Occam's 'razor': the notion that the best argument is the one that is supported by the least number of logical steps. However, the fact that to achieve the 'less is more *look*' more material was usually involved than raw construction needs would have required, proves that this was (and is) in fact an aesthetic proposition, even though not overtly argued for as such.

Aesthetics are a little like ethics in this regard. You have an aesthetic position even if you do not espouse one, and a critic can describe it, trace its antecedents, and critique it. Fuksas' Venice Architecture Biennale (2000) slogan 'Less Aesthetics, More Ethics' was, in the context of this argument, essentially mischievous.[3] Probably we are condemned to have as much aesthetics as we have ethics, whatever we do. But does that mean that we should espouse an aesthetic in the interests of the 'architecture of change' and, in the pursuit of sustainable existence, adopt an aesthetic? Perhaps it does. But perhaps such adoption is needed only in a pioneering phase, and perhaps only within the context of alerting a slumbering public consciousness about the need for change.

The work of some prominent contemporary architects has specifically called upon a ruling elite to embrace change and has, thereby, consistently pursued two parallel aims: the desire to find forms and organising principles that reduce energy use, and the desire to capture the imaginations of the elites who commission buildings. In such conditions, the use of a consciously devised aesthetic seems to be part of the ethical position.

An opposite approach is that of the architectural scientists at ETH Zurich who proved that – in the specific circumstances of Switzerland – a Miesian glass pavilion had a smaller 'carbon footprint' than a contemporary version of a traditional house. Here they were balancing lifetime energy costs, the embodied energy in the materials used in construction and the effects of efficiently captured and utilised insulation. The countervailing message here is that nothing in ecologically responsible design is necessarily what it appears to be. The New Monte Rosa Hut (2002), designed for the 150th anniversary of ETH by students of the Department of Architecture and building industry specialists, follows this line of argument, and curiously adopts a Bruno Taut-like

'glass architecture' aesthetic that promotes this 'no nonsense' approach.[4] Its crystalline form, also redolent of the original ETH glass pavilion, might be said to 'aestheticise' the ethical proposition that a building is only as supportive of sustainability as it is measured to be in practice.

The Hut was entered in the 'Zumtobel Group Award for Sustainability and Humanity in the Built Environment' (2007), an award that brings together numerous building designs that purport to contribute to an architecture of change and an assemblage that affords an opportunity to discuss the aesthetic state of affairs in the realm of sustainable design. The first observation that can be made is that certain ontologies persist in the ancient art of architecture. Here, their background a slight nod to Rykwert's 'primitive hut', are designs that mimic the form of a tree, with an oversailing canopy that shades the building from the effects of the sun. The METI School in Rudrapur, Bangladesh (Anna Heringer and Elke Roswag, 2006) is a fine example, with a largely open upper storey supported by the multiple branches of a truss system that shades a lower storey of masonry. S-House by GrAT in Austria (2005) is perhaps also in this family. By contrast, The Apple Primary School in Tibet by Limited Design (2006) and Lyons Architects' DPI Queenscliffe Centre (2005) are perhaps descended from everything that we have learned during our millennia as a cave-dwelling species, seeking out the shelter of massive overhangs and the thermal comfort that can be derived from the stasis of that mass. Conceptually at least, these buildings are – as Rassmussen argued – carved out of mass.[5] Descended from our history as weavers (as Godfried Semper believed architecture to be[6]) are those buildings that use screens as their primary method for shielding the building from the elements: New Sidwell Friends School (2006), SIEEB (2006), United States Federal Building (2007) and INVERSAbrane (2006) are amongst those featured in this publication.

These designs 'speak' about their approach to sustainability through their form — we could describe them as being, to some extent, 'narrative architecture' that is concerned with expressing its civic responsibility. There is another set of designs that are just as responsible, some possibly more so, that are indifferent to the civic narrative of sustainability. They pursue a different aesthetic agenda even as they embody a similar ethic: the LDA and LCCA Offices at Palestra (2006) speak of being a member of Alsop's family of dramatically cantilevered urban objects including Peckham Library and the Toronto University Library. The impact is that of a structural 'Look Ma! No hands!'; the fact that these forms serve a sustainable agenda being a secondary effect. Their primary concern is to act as urban regenerators. Sauerbruch Hutton Architects' Federal Environmental Agency (2005) seems to me also to have an aesthetic that — while it certainly encompasses sustainability — is more about its position in Dessau, on a particular site, responding to an urban regeneration agenda in an old city with a distinguished design history of its own, and as part of a developing oeuvre of sinuous and colourful designs calculated to delight and uplift urban dwellers. The Howard Hughes Medical Institute (2006) is possibly also in this category, but the previous work of these architects is not well-known enough for me to be able to substantiate this claim.

The temptation to mimic what is desired was a failing of high imperial art in England, and I venture to suggest that the inverted droplet of water section that is such a distinctive feature of Steven Holl Architects' design for the Whitney Water Purification Facility and Park (2005) partakes of this desire to evoke the pathos of the subject. Ironically this can be seen as a late capitalist manifestation of the work of a romantic constructivist; Melnikov used this emotion-activating approach,[7] known to art critics as the 'pathetic fallacy,' as he strove to serve the Soviet State by telegraphing its desires for industrialisation with hugely inflated imagery of industrial compo-

nentry. His designs of factories and assembly halls relied on the hugely enlarged shapes of automobile headlights, scythes, and ball bearing rings for their rhetorical impact. Morphosis' adoption of the screen as a rhetorical scale-destroying device allied to super-graphic expressionism (see Caltrans in Los Angeles) is also redolent of Melnikov's populist aesthetic of industrialisation. However, our surprise should be moderated by the awareness that we are probably still at the stage where such a populist rhetoric is just what is needed, especially when a government or a corporation wishes to let people know that *something* is indeed being done.

Is a more inherent aesthetic of sustainability emerging? KOL/MAC LCC's INVERSAbrane (2006) takes us into newer territory. Here the emergence of new ways of visualising form and new ways of constructing form out of composites come together in an evocation of a potential future in which a building skin can be woven in three dimensions and inflected so that some of the weft is solar panel, some of the woof is solar cell, and all of it allows for permeability that affords both light or shade and a view, and the woof and weft can be tugged and distorted for dramatic effect as well. Is this an expressive aesthetic? Certainly the emerging possibilities of building skins that are three-dimensionally woven to suit particular sites and particular programmes are innovative. It refers to the tent as the more inclusive and nomadic of the architectural ontologies, and it is probably a sign of a future in which there is less need for rhetoric because the building skin programmed and woven according to need will have become ubiquitous. This would indeed be an outcome of 'less aesthetics, more ethics.'

If we attempt an ethical assessment of these aesthetic positions, we have to conclude that their 'universalisability' is still remorselessly exclusive to humankind. Given this, it is encouraging that high-tech efforts (United States Federal Building, San Francisco) and low-tech efforts (METI School,

Bangladesh) are included in the award. As to 'informed consent', we lag well behind where we ought to be. It is doubtful to what extent architects can be held accountable for the popular ignorance about the resources implications of inhabiting buildings, but the designs in this collection that aim to shift attention through their rhetoric, can be seen to move towards this end. We must hope that they are more than rhetorical works aimed at 'greening' the image of their owners.

The problem with this approach is that it suggests that Sustainability is a discipline in its own right, on a par with, and, perhaps, replacing the discipline of architecture. And yet surely this is not what is intended by architects who actively pursue a sustainability agenda in modes other than design. Perhaps the concept of literacy helps us to unravel what is at stake here. The contemporary, ethical citizen is expected to achieve and maintain literacy in language, mathematics, civil and human rights, occupational health and safety, and so on. All of these are pursued as disciplines, but citizens are expected to attain only a level of competency that supports their duties as citizens. Perhaps we can come to regard sustainability as a discipline pursued by specialists, but used as a literacy by responsible citizens, including architects.

Back in the context of the principles of ethical argument, the buildings in this set that quietly get on with being ecologically responsible, as if this were simply a 'literacy' that we should find unremarkable, are perhaps most focused on arguing not in the abstract, but using specific 'content'. The approach of Sauerbruch Hutton Architects is exemplary here. Among the literacies that we have a right to expect from works of architecture are positions on enhancing urban fabrics through shape, colour and footprint, and the building of local cultures of architecture through a consistently developing body of recognisable work that resonates with and builds local mental space. There are long histories to be acknowledged

in this approach. We should be able to take the architect's resource minimisation for granted. The work of this company evokes this kind of feeling in us.

For sheer open-ended 'generosity', it is difficult to surpass the contribution made by KOL/MAC LCC, whose experiments in the past might have seemed to be wilful formalism enabled by new technologies. Perhaps this is how we have always embraced the new: through what seems at first to be 'play' – usually prefixed with the epithet 'self-indulgent'. What is significant here is that this is 'play' with aesthetic aforethought. And it is exploration that is 'playing' into the realm of truly 'less is more' technologies of composite fibres, three-dimensional weaving on the large scale, and photoelectronic advances. The architects of the current generation who are exploring 'non-standard' approaches and who are doing this in an open-ended way are perhaps leading us into an aesthetic-ethic coupling that braids together all of our desired-for literacies: ethical, cultural and ecological.

1   Heinz von Foerster and Bernhard Poerksen (2002) *Understanding Systems: Conversations on Epistemology and Ethics.* New York, Boston, Dordrecht, London Moscow: Kluwer Academic/ Plenum Publishers.

2   Roger Scruton (1979) *The Aesthetics of Architecture.* London: Methuen & Co. Ltd.

3   Leon van Schaik, (2000). 'Less Aesthetics, More Ethics'. 7th International Architecture Exhibition, La Biennale di Venezia. Marsilio, Venice.

4   Ulrich Conrads (1970) *Programmes and Manifestoes: 20th Century Architecture.* London: Lund Humphries.

5   Steen Eiler Rasmussen (1959) *Experiencing Architecture.* London: Chapman & Hall Ltd.

6   Harry Francis Mallgrave (1996) *Gottfried Semper: Architect of the Nineteenth Century.* New Haven & London: Yale University Press.

7   S. Frederick Starr (1981) *Melnikov: Solo Architect in a Mass Society.* Princeton: Princeton University Press.

Shake the Future

Kristin Feireiss in conversation with Yung Ho Chang

Kristin Feireiss is the founder of the Aedes Architecture Forum, Berlin and editor of numerous books on architecture.

Yung Ho Chang is Professor of Architecture and Head of the Department of Architecture at the Massachusetts Institute of Technology (MIT).

KF   You are one of China's most accomplished contemporary architects, founding head of the Graduate Centre of Architecture at Peking University and head of MIT's Department of Architecture. In your work as practising architect and educator you promote reflection, learning and debate about new possibilities and directions in architecture. Against the threatening backdrop of possible climate crisis, environmentally responsible design is obviously one of these new directions in contemporary architecture. Today green architecture is popular as never before. But what is sustainable architecture really, and what is your assessment of this development in contemporary architecture?

YHC   Less then a generation ago, the popular imagery of sustainable building was associated with rather uninspired designs that put environmental concerns in conflict with artistic ones. Today, some design architects have turned to green architecture and have proven that eco-friendly architecture by no means fails to win in the aesthetic realm.

While sustainable architecture is not easy to define, the issues that concern climate change, such as energy and pollution, are very real. Architectural practice has no choice but to respond to them. Sustainability could be a matter of degree: some buildings and cities will be more sustainable than others. However, every effort towards sustainability counts, every small step matters. A design that reduces only a fraction of the typical energy consumption is better than none. What is also important for architects to realise when pursuing sustainability is the design opportunity: the measures we take to go green may also reshape the way we perceive space and form. I am confident more and more architects will catch up with this new frontier of architecture.

KF   As head of MIT's Department of Architecture, you strongly influence new generations of architects by preparing them for the future. What emphasis do you place on archi-

tectural education? What role do questions of sustainability play at MIT and how are they implemented in the architecture programme's curriculum?

YHC   Today, architects are confronted with four contemporary conditions that were not major issues in the previous eras: climate change, globalisation, rapid urbanisation, and new technology. Therefore, these concerns have to be built into the design curriculum. While faculty members here may or may not agree with me, and we constantly debate on architecture and education, the Architecture Department of MIT (the oldest department of architecture in the United States) is going through tremendous changes. The old curricula at MIT will no longer be adequate. We have embarked on a substantial reform of our programmes. As far as climate change, from next academic year, we will try to bring building technology further towards the centre of design culture and have regular studios that address the climate change. In the autumn semester of 2008, we will also have a lecture series on the relationship between sustainability and design. Research and design activities in the area of eco-urbanism are also being planned.

Meanwhile, we intend to actively develop diversity and interdisciplinarity, a trademark of our department, and further integrate the five discipline groups within the department: building technology, computation, design (including urbanism), history theory and criticism and the visual arts. As always, we will maintain a highly international faculty as well as student body. With our students and faculty, we are building programmes around global agendas and continue to pursue design/research activities in many parts of the world.

KF   You are also a member of the jury of the first Zumtobel Group Award on Sustainability and Humanity in the Built Environment upon whose research this publication is based. What could be learned from the jury session?

YHC   First of all, the jury distinguished itself through its international and interdisciplinary line-up. The members of the jury comprised outstanding international architects and theorists, a leading engineer, a philosopher, an economist and a United Nations secretary. This is not the common procedure for architectural awards but it makes a lot of sense to bring together people from very diverse academic and professional backgrounds. The issues discussed at the Zumtobel Group Award concern all of us: sustainability and humanity in the built environment. The latter I would rather interpret as the general living conditions in the city. The question therefore is what we can do to improve these conditions for the future. This surely is not merely a challenge for architects and city planners. The same accounts for sustainability, which is not a mere technical issue. It is also something bigger than architecture and design. It was very interesting and important to hear certain concerns being addressed from different angles. The kind of interdisciplinarity at this jury should become a standard practise in the future.

We gave last year's award almost unanimously to Thom Mayne, a well-known figure within the architectural world, because we believe that his project best addressed the discussed issues. Mayne has combined leading-edge sustainable technology with intelligent design strategies to create an architectural landmark of great aesthetic quality and will hopefully have considerable impact on sustainable architectural design worldwide. But perhaps in the future, younger practises will receive awards; this would strengthen the message to stimulate and encourage architects to work further in this field. In the next Zumtobel Group Award, it will be interesting to see if there are even more works situated between the low-tech, rural approach and the major, signature kind of architecture. We do see signs of a new architecture in many of the projects, which showed a great deal of sophistication. What I would be curious to see, however, is an architect like Thom Mayne designing a little school in Bangladesh, or vice-versa, a more folksy, vernacular architect taking on a skyscraper.

In general, I hope that the Zumtobel Group Award will become an opportunity for architects and academics to really shake up the future of architecture.

KF   As a Chinese architect educated both in China and the United States and living and working in the United States, you constantly embrace two different cultures and backgrounds. What steps do you see being taken towards sustainable design in the built environment in China?

YHC   In China, climate change was the number one item on the agenda at the recent national congress of the Communist party. With the push of the government, one can expect more discussions, if not actions, to be taken to save energy and reduce pollution. China has had an energy code for building for some years, although how it is reinforced is not entirely clear. Hopefully, serious and effective measures will be carried out in China and improvements made. Sustainability definitely involves a level of technology and even more importantly, a certain attitude.

Without question, the awareness of sustainability is there now. It is almost popular for the media to talk about it. However in reality, it is not quite yet believed. The speed of developments and the lack of expertise in certain building technologies mean that it is still rather difficult to implement sustainable ideas into many projects. I have had some experience myself with clients who suggested exploring issues of sustainability and then ultimately refrained from implementing our proposals because they were considered too expensive and not realisable over a short period of time. So these ideas were left behind and we followed the conventions. In the long-term, I am more optimistic, and the long-term could come around very soon.

KF   The world we are living in is constantly changing at an ever-increasing pace. Where do you see the future of architectural performance and what are the new frontiers and challenges in architecture and beyond?

YHC   Besides climate change, globalisation, rapid urbanisation, and new technology will all have a decisive impact on architecture. Buildings and cities will be transformed in the process. While everything is rather open-ended right now, cutting-edge architectural design will definitely shift from its focus on aesthetics to playing a greater role in the betterment of the living environment.

This development can already be seen today. With the issues of humanity and sustainability, we see the divide between vernacular architecture and high-style, iconic architecture being blurred if not totally removed. As an architect, I like to think that in future most architectural practises will be able to position their work, not in either camp but between the two.

Projects

S-House

Research & Education Centre
Böheimkirchen, Austria
2005

GrAT - Centre
for Appropriate
Technology

University of Technology, Vienna
Vienna, Austria

↘ 143 | The S-House combines passive house technology, renewable resources and regional available materials in a modular and contemporary architectural design.

The main challenge of the Straw Bale House (S-House) project was to develop a replicable design for buildings, which reduce the environmental impact of the average home by a factor of ten. This enormous resource efficiency should comprise the whole life cycle of the building and its use. These goals were achieved through a systematic approach that combines passive house technology, renewable resources and regionally available materials in a modular and contemporary architectural design.

All sustainable development criteria are to be met at the highest level; this also applies to economic viability. The results of this project would help the construction industry to solve current problems with construction waste, hazardous materials and a high level of energy consumption. In order to demonstrate the feasibility of the concept, the building was extensively tested at the Centre for Appropriate Technology at the Vienna University of Technology.

The concept combines contemporary architecture with traditional building materials like wood, straw or clay as well as with highly innovative solutions like biopolymers and biomimetic construction principles.

Comparison of the environmental performance of straw bale construction and conventional constructions has shown improved values up to a factor of ten.

The design concept separates technical and biological material cycles. The house technology is modular and can be easily maintained, updated and removed while the building shell is completely renewable and biodegradable at the end of its useful life. Project documentation and education will take place via a multimedia exhibition and website. The S-House is open to the public for seminars or other informative events.

The use of appropriate technology criteria means that social and cultural aspects are included on an equal footing with technical aspects during the development process. Transferability into other cultural and climatic conditions has been taken into consideration.

A consistent systematic approach using detailed planning and implementation has resulted in a number of technical innovations that work together to achieve the overall goal, such as: minimal excavation, reuse for clay plaster and rainwater retention on the lightweight green membranous roof. An earth heat exchanger for balancing temperature has furthermore been implemented, as well as a special biomass stove that sends heat through the ventilation system using staggered timing. The building shell is made of renewable materials like wood, straw and clay. The energy supply is provided solely from solar radiation and biomass. The costs are comparable to those of conventional buildings. Added

value for regional agricultural products (e.g. straw bale insulation) can be attained. The house has low maintenance costs and heating cost. The extremely low demolition costs after use, due to biodegradable untreated materials, are also of note. Valuable materials and modules of the house technology can be easily reused in other buildings.

The S-House serves as a centre for sustainable technology, renewable raw materials and sustainable building technologies. The components and designed structures are presented to visitors, and therefore, traditional expertise and recent developments in the construction industry thus become accessible to the public. In addition to exhibitions, other events like symposiums, workshops and advanced learning sessions take place.

[1]

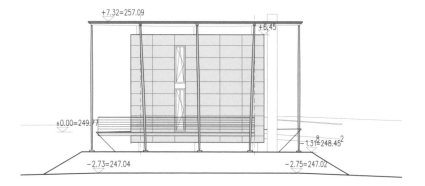

[2]

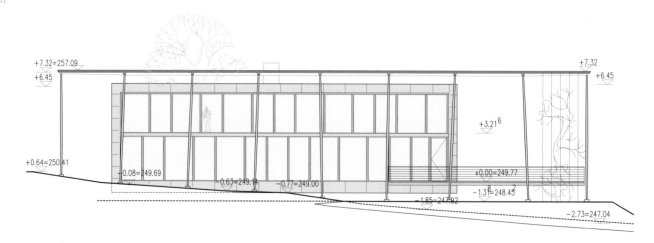

[3]

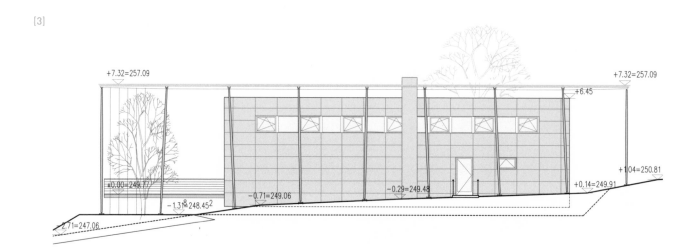

[1] | East elevation
[2] | South elevation
[3] | North elevation
[4] | South elevation of the building. The house technology is modular and can be easily maintained, updated and removed while the building shell is purely renewable and biodegradable.
[5] | Building process
[6] | Interiour view

[4]

[5]

[6]

project

METI School

School Building
Rudrapur, Bangladesh
2005

architects

Anna Herringer,
Eike Roswag

Berlin, Germany

147

| Front elevation of the handmade
METI School in the northern part
of Bangladesh.

[1]

[2]

[3]

[1] [2] | The moulded 'cavespaces' provide an
area to retreat into for contemplation
and concentrated work.

[3] | Interiour view of a class room.
The thick walls assure a comfortable
climate on the ground floor of the
building.

The Modern Education and Training Institute (METI) School was built by local craftsmen, pupils and teachers together with a European team of volunteers in Rudrapur in Bangladesh. Rudrapur is a typical Bengali village in the north of the country, which is one of the poorest areas in Bangladesh. Almost 60% of the families are landless; no more than 22% population in the area have access to electricity; the unemployment rate is very high and acute. As agriculture is the main activity, there are no other opportunities for employment and income generation throughout the year.

In order to respond to this situation, the concept had to provide a construction method that mainly required human labour and to use a suitable technique that was easy for the villagers to learn, but which solved the problems of the general living conditions, which include short longevity of about fifteen years, dark and humid rooms, an uncomfortable indoor climate and fungus.

The philosophy of METI is enjoyment of learning. The teachers help the children to develop their own potential and to use it in a creative and responsible way. The building reflects these ideas

[1]

[2]

[3]

[4]

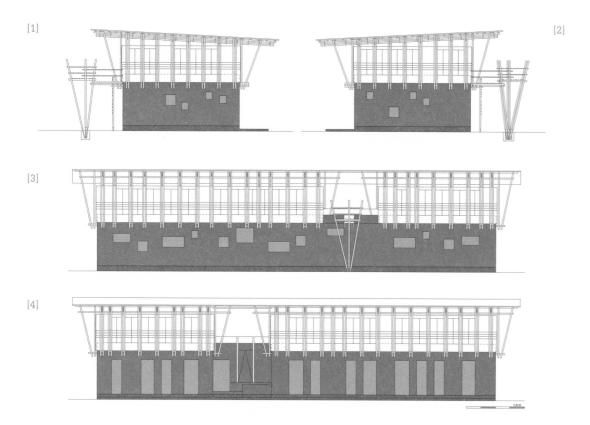

1.0 m

[5]

[7]

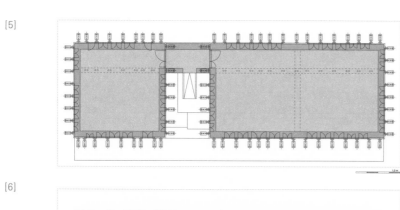

1.0 m

[6]

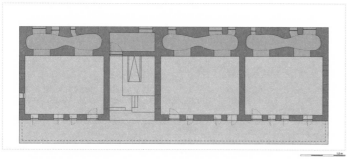

1.0 m

[1] | South elevation
[2] | North elevation
[3] | West elevation
[4] | East elevation
[5] | Upper floor plan
[6] | Ground floor plan
[7] | North-east elevation. Air
       conditioning is not needed since
       the natural airflow and the thick
       loam walls regulate the indoor
       climate at a comfortable level.

in terms of materials, techniques and architectural design. The aim of the project was to improve existing construction techniques, to maintain sustainability by utilising local potential and to strengthen regional identity. The challenge of the project was to meet the needs and dreams of the people in an economically reasonable, ecological, social and aesthetic way. The strategy was the development of knowledge, information and skills for the optimal use of locally available resources, respecting existing culture but also applying it in a modern manner. In Bangladesh, the building materials of earth and bamboo are viewed as 'old-fashioned' and as 'materials for the poor'. As a representative public building in a modern architectural style, the school was a first step towards rethinking this image.

The METI School was built using manual labour: the bamboo came by ox and cart, the straw by rickshaw. No crane was available to lift the bamboo construction, people transported loam on their head in baskets and the mixing machine was drawn by water buffaloes. The only exceptions were the loam, which was collected by tractor, but from very close by (3 km) and the drills, which were charged by electric power. Since the beginning of May 2007, solar panels have been producing electricity to light the building and to provide energy for some technical equipment. This project displays the successful symbiosis of older traditional, low-tech building materials with high-tech and new technology concepts. Air conditioning is not necessary since the natural airflow and the thick

loam walls maintain the indoor climate at a comfortable level.

With the exception of some steel pins and the corrugated iron sheets, the construction was based on materials, mainly earth and bamboo, that do not require any electricity during their production. These materials therefore do not create any ecological debt to the ecosystem.

Bamboo even contributes to the reduction of climate change. At present, approximately 20 per cent of the houses in rural areas are built from bricks, the rest are bamboo/straw or loam buildings. If Bangladesh continues the present trend in its rural areas and follows the global model in investing in brick houses,

152

the result would be a tremendous increase in CO2 emissions due to coal, the energy source of the brickfields. Building with loam is an excellent way of preventing an increase in a country's ecological footprint and is affordable even for the poorest members of a developing country.

The local materials also offer advantages from an economic point of view: they strengthen the local economy and create jobs. The bamboo, for example, was cultivated by local peasants. All the workers came from the village of Rudrapur. The construction process was linked with training, in order to build up knowledge of sustainable architecture. In order for the project to have lasting impact, it was essential that local workers were included in the construction processes. Training through 'learning by

doing' should help local craftspeople to improve their general housing conditions. Not only the villagers but also the METI pupils and teachers were included in the construction process. The participatory approach was beneficial to all participants: pupils and teachers, villagers / builders and the European team of architects, craftspeople and students. In many ways – intercultural understanding, creativity and craftsmanship, for example – this was a mutual learning process.

↘ 152 | Interiour view of the upper floor
↘ 153 | Elegantly fusing local knowledge, readily available renewable materials and new construction techniques, the project maintains a traditional identity while embracing modernity in both its form and purpose.

Ali Apple
Elementary
School

School Building
Ali, Tibet
2006 (ongoing)

Limited Design

Beijng, China

The Ali Apple Elementary School, sponsored by the donations contributed from the Apple Education Fund, sits at an elevation of 4,800 metres and is located at the base of a sacred Buddhist mountain.

The concept of the initial design is to promote architecture to have a natural ecological relationship with the environment, enable the children to have an abundance of full experiences within the space and introduce contemporaneous aspects into the architecture. Due to the high altitude, the choice of local construction material was minimal and therefore a decisive factor even before the project had started. There was an abundance of cobblestone, which could be used in large quantities. Stone is used all over Tibet in construction; in many places stones are piled up to create storage pens for livestock . Further examples of the various economising aspects of the design and the construction are the cobblestone concrete-type block material that was created in large amounts and was closely integrated and combined with the new body of the construction as well as the original base, like a kind of growth.

The walls play an essential role: they provide shelter from the wind. On average, there are 149 days of windy weather each year; in the western mountain valley of Ali Daerqin's hinterland, wind and sun are two of the most important and influential elements that need to

be considered before construction can take place. On a windless day, even if it is -20° to -30°C, local people still prefer to sit outside in the sun. The original idea of varying the space between the groups of walls intended to support this kind of outdoor enjoyment: the windless courtyard lets in the rays from the sun so that people can enjoy the beauty and splendour of the outdoors.

The shape of the walls and space between them is irregular and derived from research on original Tibetan architecture. The height and the distance of walls within a Tibetan courtyard were formed specifically to solve problems posed by wind and security. The Tibetan courtyards are multidimensional, but the width of the houses and the size of the courtyard and its walls have a specific relationship. Like the folds within an accordion, the walls of the courtyard are flexible and so facilitate future development and change.

↘ ⏐ The irregularly shaped walls cobble together with the topography and disappear at the base of the structure.

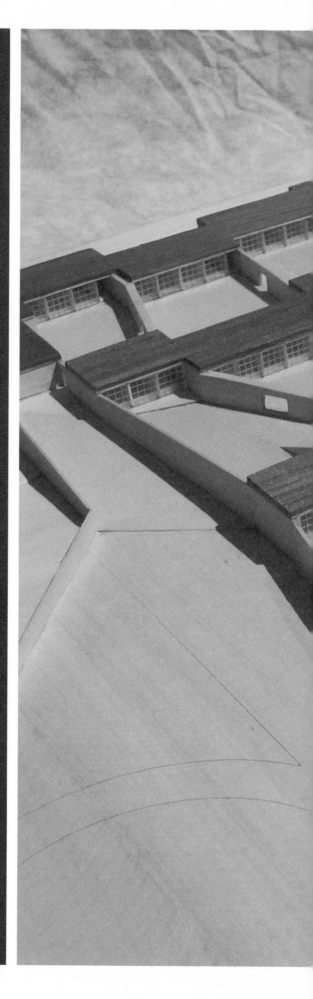

[1] | View of the surrounding landscape
[2] | The school sits at an elevation of
        4,800 metres and is located at the
        base of a sacred Buddhist mountain.
[3] | The inner courtyards offer
        protection from the strong prevailing
        winds.

Ultimately, the irregularly shaped walls
fit into the topography and disappear at
the base of the structure. More importantly, with the walls now acting as a
barrier to the wind, people's attention
is drawn towards the sacred mountain,
which is portrayed as the centre of the
universe and is part of this region's
unique landscape.

All the buildings within the courtyard
face south. Due to the lack of any electric energy, the southern exposure allowed for full utilisation of solar energy
from the sun. The entire south wall
is a double-layer steel-framed glass
window. This was designed to improve
solar energy efficiency by integrating
transparency, ventilation and heating.
Black corrugated iron was placed between the double-glazed windows that
face south. During the day, after the
sun's rays have heated the iron up, the

hot air produced is sufficient to meet
heating requirements.

If it becomes too hot, the double-glazed
glass is opened to form a convection
current, where hot air escapes. This is
similar to a Tibetan robe that consists of
half sleeves that facilitate heat adjustment. The utilisation of wind energy
and how to convert wind into electricity was also an important element of
the design. The problem was that even
a simple windmill installation would
destroy the natural environment of the
area, so a small, propelling 'wind tunnel'
was installed instead. The requirements
of the structural design and its final outcome were completed by using the most
economical methods possible.

[1]   [2]

[3]

Sidwell Friends Middle School

KieranTimberlake Associates

School Building
Washington, DC, USA
2006

Philadelphia, USA

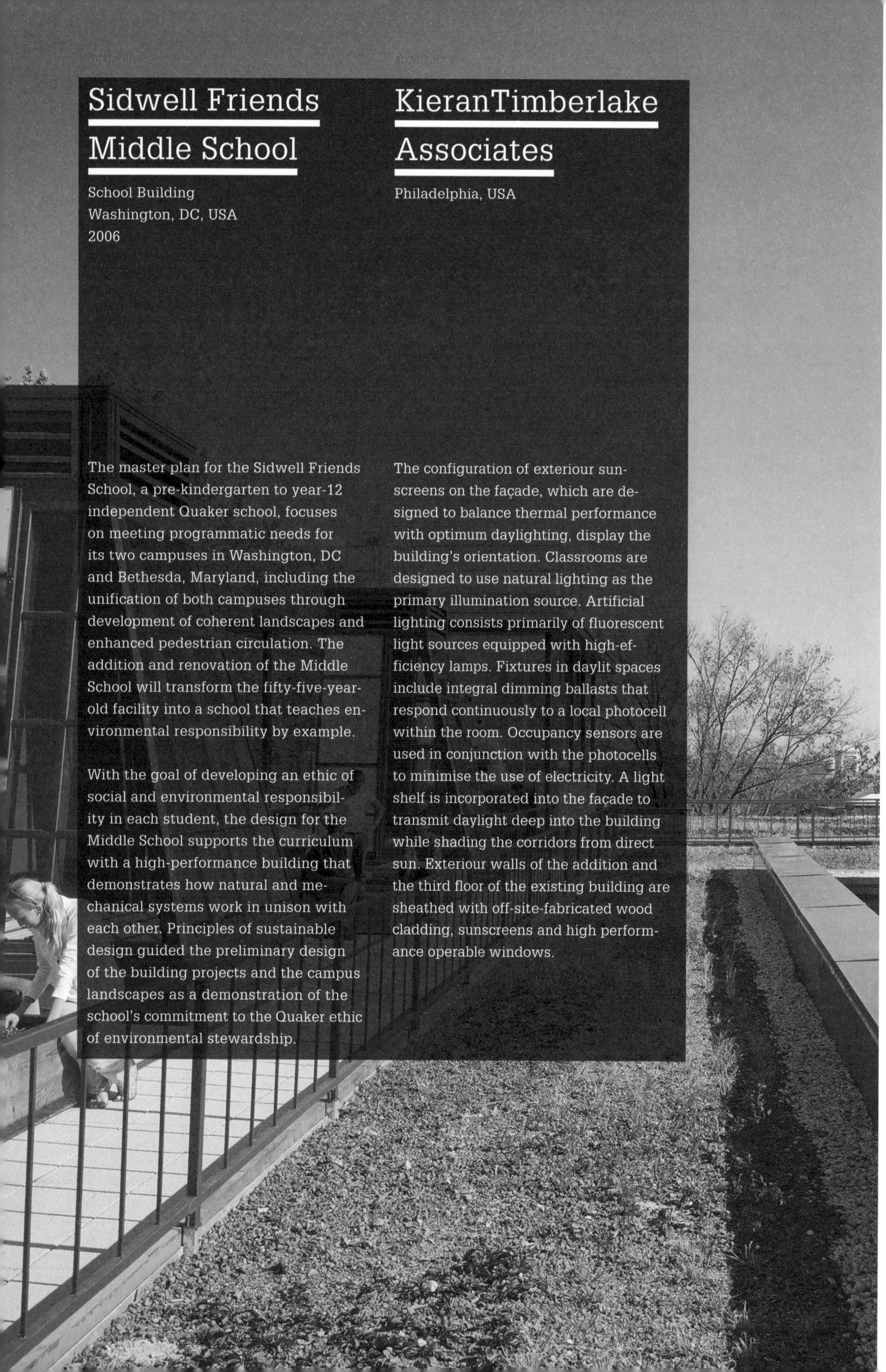

The master plan for the Sidwell Friends School, a pre-kindergarten to year-12 independent Quaker school, focuses on meeting programmatic needs for its two campuses in Washington, DC and Bethesda, Maryland, including the unification of both campuses through development of coherent landscapes and enhanced pedestrian circulation. The addition and renovation of the Middle School will transform the fifty-five-year-old facility into a school that teaches environmental responsibility by example.

With the goal of developing an ethic of social and environmental responsibility in each student, the design for the Middle School supports the curriculum with a high-performance building that demonstrates how natural and mechanical systems work in unison with each other. Principles of sustainable design guided the preliminary design of the building projects and the campus landscapes as a demonstration of the school's commitment to the Quaker ethic of environmental stewardship.

The configuration of exteriour sunscreens on the façade, which are designed to balance thermal performance with optimum daylighting, display the building's orientation. Classrooms are designed to use natural lighting as the primary illumination source. Artificial lighting consists primarily of fluorescent light sources equipped with high-efficiency lamps. Fixtures in daylit spaces include integral dimming ballasts that respond continuously to a local photocell within the room. Occupancy sensors are used in conjunction with the photocells to minimise the use of electricity. A light shelf is incorporated into the façade to transmit daylight deep into the building while shading the corridors from direct sun. Exteriour walls of the addition and the third floor of the existing building are sheathed with off-site-fabricated wood cladding, sunscreens and high performance operable windows.

Exteriour walls are sheathed with off-site-fabricated wood cladding, sunscreens and high performance operable windows.

[1] | Solar chimneys and container
gardens on the roof serve as an
outdoor classroom.
[2] | A walkway at the entry to the building
overlooks the constructed wetland.
[3] | A constructed wetland at the
campus-side entry forecourt treats
and recycles all building wastewater
for grey water use within the building.

| Water collection diagramm

Solar chimneys are designed for mechanically assisted natural ventilation to minimise the need for artificial cooling. The central air system is designed to take advantage of economiser operation to minimise the mechanical treatment of outside air, and includes energy recovery to minimise waste of mechanical heating and cooling. A constructed wetland at the campus-side entry forecourt treats and recycles all building wastewater for grey water use within the building, resulting in a 94 per cent reduction of municipal water use.

Landscape areas have been converted from lawns to 'micro-restoration' areas. More than eighty regionally appropriate native species were introduced into the campus landscape.

The collection and diversion of rainwater through the vegetated roof reduces stormwater runoff. A series of flow forms direct rainwater to a biology pond and rain garden that supports the native habitat and serves as a programmatic component of the science curriculum. The vegetated roof retains stormwater and reduces the 'heat island' effect characteristic of conventional roofing. A central energy plant serves the entire campus, allowing greater efficiency and control of energy resources. Five per cent of the overall building's electrical load is generated by photovoltaic panels.

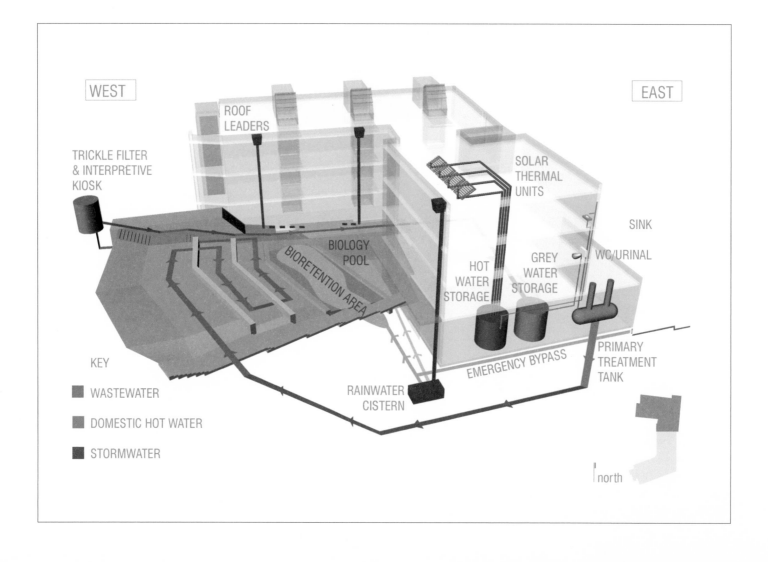

[1] | An incorporated light shelf in the façade transmits daylight deep into the building while shading the corridors from direct sun.

[2] | The configuration of exteriour sunscreens on the façade is designed to balance the thermal performance with optimum day lighting.

[1]

[2]

Building materials are reused, recycled, are rapidly renewable and/or regionally acquired, including reclaimed wood cladding for the façade. Reclaimed materials include exterior cladding made from reclaimed red cedar fermentation barrels, greenheart flooring and decking from pilings in the Baltimore Harbor, and all of the stone to construct the wetland and other outdoor stone walks and walls.

Interiour finishes were selected for their high levels of recycled content. During the demolition of the interiour of the existing building, three waste bins were provided for the sorting of materials for recycling. At all other times during the construction, waste was collected and taken to an off-site location for sorting to reduce the amount of waste that entered landfills.

project

DPI Queenscliff
Centre

Research Centre
Queenscliff, Australia
2005

architects

Lyons Architects

Melbourne, Australia

↘ | The landscape literally wraps up and over the roof, merging the building with the surrounding area.

The DPI Queenscliff Centre is the peak research institute for the State of Victoria, Australia relating to marine environment research. The project site for the new research institute is a narrow bridge of land linking a coastal township with the major regional peninsula. The site overlooks Swan Bay, which was designated a World Heritage Marine Park in 1999. The site was also a former 'rubbish dump', and a number of significant contaminations had to be managed by the project design.

The building is a demonstration project incorporating high-end environmental design objectives within a complex architectural form and design strategy.

This project responds to each of the major global issues regarding environmental management: protecting fragile coastal environments, rehabilitating local ecologies, reversing contamination of the soil, harvesting water in a sustainable way, cleaning water runoffs before they re-enter natural ecologies, and significantly reducing the energy requirements for a building of this type.

The architects took a holistic approach to integrating environmental design into the conceptual architectural design-thinking and form–making; numerous site 'constraints' were in fact reinterpreted as design opportunities.

↘ | Site plan.
1 Support Building, 2 Offices,
3 Conference/entry, 4 Laboratories,
5 Marine Discovery Centre,
6 Stormwater wetland

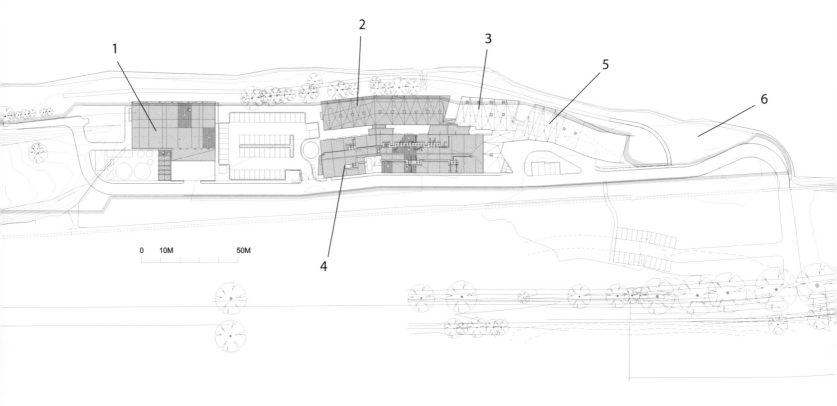

The site design response, architectural form, building structure, environmental systems and landscape design are all fully integrated into the final project design and building form. Although the project foregrounds the environmental design attributes of the building, it also responds directly to a range of other design issues: formal, cultural and site-related.

In doing so, the design goes beyond simply targeting energy saving and creates best practice across a wide spectrum of environmental initiatives including building design, use of indigenous landscaping, storm water management, rehabilitation of local ecologies, use of materials and minimising the visual impact.

As regards the scale of the site, the project has rehabilitated an important section of the coastal environment and has been built in such a way as to protect the area from future degradation, to maintain biodiversity by the construction of wetlands and the planting of indigenous plants (60,000 plants).

The building has an optimal north-facing orientation, maximising passive solar design and shading. It is designed as a thermal mass, created through a concrete structure, which is insulated by a landscaped roof. This design concept allows primary areas within the building to be fully naturally ventilated.

The roof landscape provides an additional landscape ecology for the site and provides nesting areas for migratory coastal birds.

A series of internal courtyards, planned within the building, provide sheltered external space during the winter months, together with providing increasing natural light and ventilation for the office areas and laboratory environments. The landscape roof provides a dual reading for the project: on the one hand, merging with the landscape and literally 'disappearing' into the site, and on the other, creating a unique and meaningful identity for the environmental science research institute.

The form of the building is also created directly from environmental design–thinking, such as the sloping wall to the façade overlooking Swan Bay, where a sloping wall shelf-shades the summer sun angles, while allowing the winter sun to heat the building directly. The interiour of the building was made from recycled materials wherever possible.

[1] | The new wetland cleans the stormwater runoff before it is returned to the adjacent bay.

[2] | The fully landscaped roof provides insulation to the building and rehabilitates indigenous vegetation.

[1]

[2]

[1]

[2]

[3]

[1] | Entrance situation
[2] | View of façade from the sea side
[3] | Office spaces

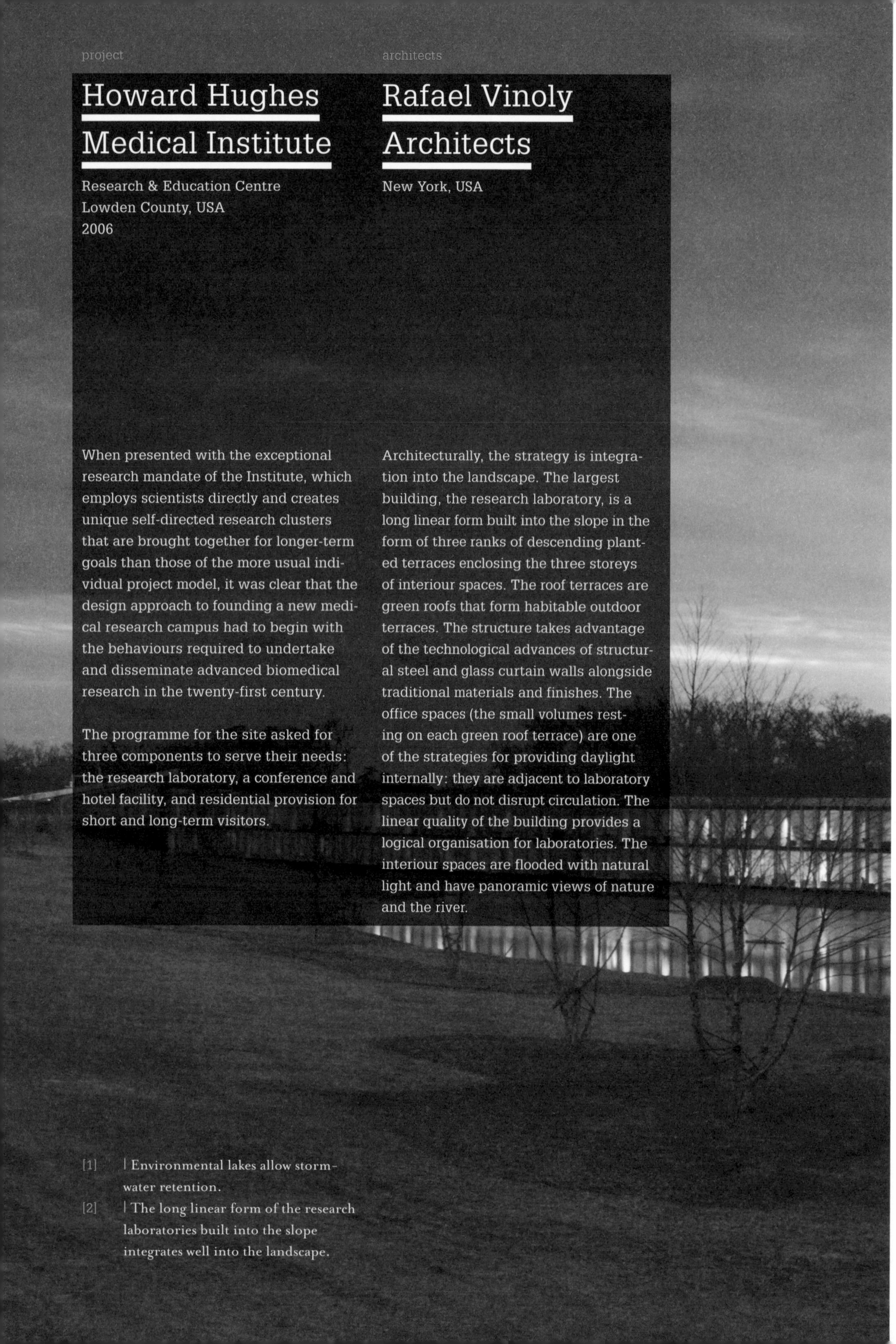

Howard Hughes
Medical Institute

Research & Education Centre
Lowden County, USA
2006

Rafael Vinoly
Architects

New York, USA

[1]

[2]

When presented with the exceptional research mandate of the Institute, which employs scientists directly and creates unique self-directed research clusters that are brought together for longer-term goals than those of the more usual individual project model, it was clear that the design approach to founding a new medical research campus had to begin with the behaviours required to undertake and disseminate advanced biomedical research in the twenty-first century.

The programme for the site asked for three components to serve their needs: the research laboratory, a conference and hotel facility, and residential provision for short and long-term visitors.

Architecturally, the strategy is integration into the landscape. The largest building, the research laboratory, is a long linear form built into the slope in the form of three ranks of descending planted terraces enclosing the three storeys of interiour spaces. The roof terraces are green roofs that form habitable outdoor terraces. The structure takes advantage of the technological advances of structural steel and glass curtain walls alongside traditional materials and finishes. The office spaces (the small volumes resting on each green roof terrace) are one of the strategies for providing daylight internally: they are adjacent to laboratory spaces but do not disrupt circulation. The linear quality of the building provides a logical organisation for laboratories. The interiour spaces are flooded with natural light and have panoramic views of nature and the river.

[1] | Environmental lakes allow storm-
         water retention.
[2] | The long linear form of the research
         laboratories built into the slope
         integrates well into the landscape.

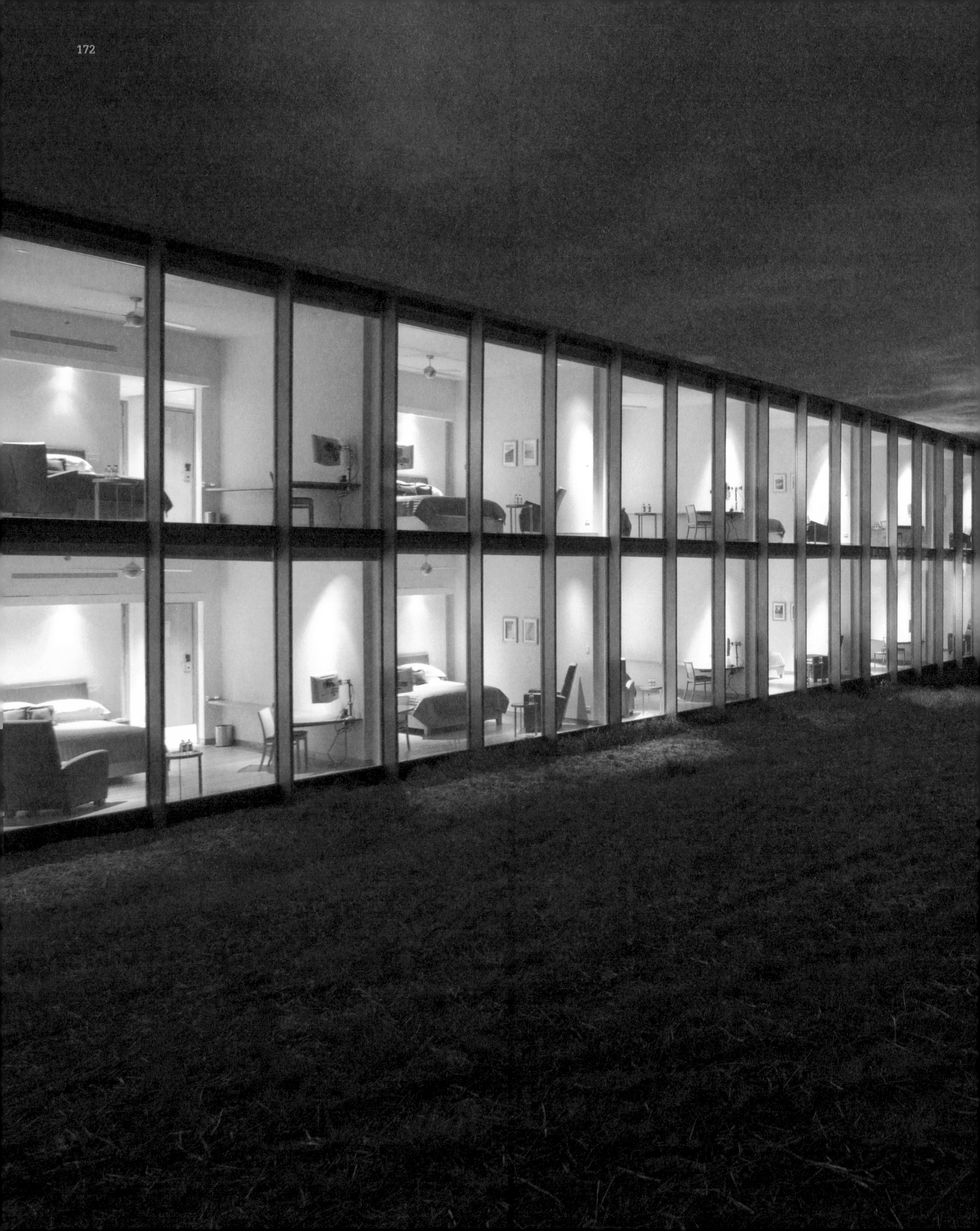

↘ | The building also provides a hotel facility and residential provision for short and long-term visitors.

The Landscape Building is not a megastructure, it is an environmentally responsible answer to a laboratory suitable for the twenty-first century. In spite of its size, the building blends into the existing trees and topography and is not visible from the highway-side approach. The success of the design is defined by the highly adaptive and flexible spaces that ensure the building's permanence, reducing the need for additional buildings that further diminish natural resources and disturb the landscape. The laboratories are designed to be adaptable to a variety of computational or office functions without requiring costly, time-consuming renovations. With a patented casework system, each laboratory can be reconfigured within a matter of hours without the need for plumbers, carpenters, electricians or supplementary building materials.

The site is planned with ease of interaction in mind. The campus itself is pedestrian-oriented and also provides bicycle storage racks. All parking spaces are below-grade. Use of materials and the sustainability of the design are based on a ground-up approach to working on the site. On-site resources were used and reused wherever possible.

[1]

[2]

[3]

[1] | Interiour view hallway
[2] | Entrance situation
[3] | Conference hall

During the build itself, all of the trees removed on-site were used as interiour materials, and all the rock removed during site preparation became aggregate for concrete or was used as ballast. A concrete plant was constructed on-site to eliminate the need for road freight to transport concrete from off-site plants. Sustainable choices were made through the full process of the build, when new materials were used, they were specified carefully: low-emittance glazing is used to reduce heat gain, LED street lights reduce maintenance and energy consumption, fast-growing bamboo is used for flooring, and sustainable wood species were selected for panelling and trim. Low-volatile organic content paints and carpets and products with recycled content were chosen. Recycled content on a larger scale is integrated throughout; incorporated into the casework, laboratory bench, ceiling tiles, and steel.

[1] | Cross-sections
[2] | The research laboratory is built into
        the slope in form of three ranks of
        descending planted outdoor terraces.
[3] | The building blends into the
        existing trees and topograhy and is
        not visible from the highway-side
        approach.

The landscaping is also sensitive to the
site, with native plant species used to
reduce maintenance and water consumption on the green roofs. The green roof
and environmental lakes affect the heating and cooling efficiency of the site and
allow stormwater retention. The lighting
provision uses several passive strategies.
The general architectural strategy itself,
with the buildings embedded into the
site, reduces temperature variations and
provides insulation and so reduces the
environmental load of the project.

The overall ethos is an integrated approach to sustainability from the small-
est details of light fixtures to the major
issue of confronting how to programme
in adaptability for unknown future
needs, without designing in the need
to demolish or build further. The goal of
creating an appropriate and beautiful
site for this exceptional research setting
has been addressed with as holistic an
approach as possible through the harnessing of past experience and the use
of leading-edge technologies.

[1]

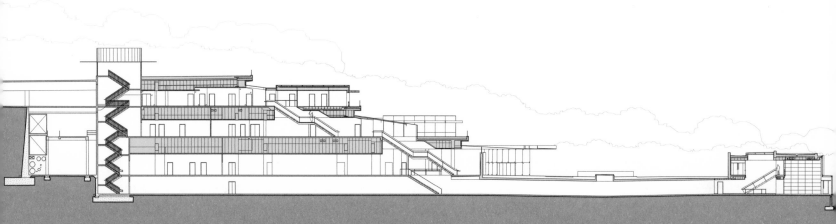

[2]

[3]

project

SIEEB

Research Centre
Beijing, China
2006

architects

Mario Cucinella
Architects

Bologna, Italy

The Sino-Italian Ecology and Energy
Building (SIEEB) is a faculty building
located on the Tsinghua University
Campus in Beijing. It houses the Sino-
Italian training and research centre for
environmental protection and energy
conservation. The building design
aims to find a balance between energy efficiency targets, minimum CO_2
emissions, a functional layout and the
concept of a contemporary building.

It is the result of cooperation between
the Ministry for Environment and
Territory of the Republic of Italy and
the Ministry of Science and Technology
of the People's Republic of China. It
is a platform for the development of
bilateral long-term cooperation between the two countries in the fields
of energy and the environment and is a
showcase for the potential for reducing
CO_2 emissions in the construction sector in China.

↘ | The open and transparent south
façade.

[1] | Green spaces, gardens and terraces
are distinctive elements of the
research centre.
[2] [3] | The building is closed and well
insulated on the norhern side, that
faces the cold winter winds, and it is
more open towards the south.

The building is closed and well-insulated on the north side, that faces the cold winter winds, and is more transparent and open towards the south side. On the east and west sides, light and direct sun are controlled by a double skin façade that filters solar gain and optimises the penetration of daylight into the office spaces. Attractive green spaces, gardens and terraces are distinctive elements of the project. Cantilevered structural elements extend to the south, giving shade to the terraces.

The shape of the SIEEB building grew from an analysis of the site and of the climatic conditions of the city of Beijing. This shape evolved from a series of tests and simulations on solar radiation and overshadowing; its expected energy performances were a major influential factor. The main starting points for the design team were a symmetrical U-shaped courtyard building that steps downwards towards the south in order to maximise sun penetration into the internal spaces and to bring light and air into the internal garden.

The external envelope of the building plays a key role in the environmental strategy, in that different solutions respond to different orientations. The building is conceived as a protective shell towards the north, while being open to the south towards the sun. The north-facing façade, which contains the main entrance from the campus, is designed to be almost entirely opaque and highly insulated to protect the building from the strong cold winter winds. Different systems of ventilated façades are used in the internal skin, facing the garden, and in the east and west outer envelope. The south-facing façades, shaded by the cantilevering floors and structures, are more transparent. The east and west-facing façades of the building are clad with a double skin composed of a simple curtain wall, based on a pattern of transparent/opaque modules and an external silk-screen façade. Horizontal lines at different densities lend the building an elegant appearance and, at the same time, contribute to the environmental control of the internal spaces.

[1]

[2]

[3]

The inner envelope, facing the internal courtyard, has a double skin composed of a simple curtain-wall system, based on the same modularity as the outer façades, and also has an external layer of glass louvers. The louvers are composed of reflective glass panes, tilted at different angles in order to control direct solar radiation and light penetration into the office spaces. Photovoltaic panels that produce energy are integrated into the design as shading elements for the terraces.

The main aim of all the services in SIEEB is to reduce energy consumption and to create comfortable conditions. The following main technologies are applied in this project: a trigeneration system, absorption, high-efficiency condensation boilers, VAV boxes, radiant ceilings, photovoltaic panels and a building management system. The combination of this equipment and these technological systems with the shape, orientation, materials and high-performance façades of the building allows a significant reduction of energy consumption and therefore of CO2 emissions.

↘ | Photovoltaic panels are integrated
into the design of the cantilevered
shading elements.

Whitney Water Purification Facility and Park

Water Purification Facility
New Haven, CT, USA
2005

Steven Holl Architects

New York, USA

↘ | The long stainless steel building or 'sliver' houses the extensive operational facilities, an exhibition lobby, laboratories, a lecture hall and conferences spaces.

This water purification plant and park make use of water and its purification process as the guiding metaphor for their design. The programme consists of water treatment facilities located beneath a public park, and a 109-metre-long stainless steel sliver that encloses the client's public and operational programmes. Like an inverted drop of water, the sliver expresses the workings of the plant below. Its shape creates a curvilinear interiour space open to a large window view of the surrounding landscape, while its exterior reflects the horizon in the landscape. The interiour facilities include an exhibition lobby, laboratories, a lecture hall, conference spaces, and extensive operational facilities.

The public park is comprised of six sectors that are analogous to the six stages of the water treatment in the plant. The change in scale from molecular scale of the purification process below ground to the landscape above is celebrated in an interpretation of microscopic morphologies as landscape sectors. The park's micro to macro reinterpretation results in unexpected and challenging material-spatial aspects.

Located near a well-developed neighbourhood, the facility occupies the over six hectare site of the previous water-treatment plant. With the aim of maintaining a park-like atmosphere, as opposed to an industrial one, the project team conceived and executed the project as a public park. The Regional Water Authority in New Haven, Connecticut (RWA) engaged

the local community in the design process as well as in the selection of the architect. RWA initiated neighbourhood design, environmental and construction committees, which met the design team regularly throughout the project.

The facility was designed for public tours, including school trips and was intended as part of an educational programme about the importance of water as a natural resource. The lobby was designed to double as an exhibition space, and a small auditorium was designed to provide a venue to show a video about the purification process and water conservation. These programmes may be implemented in the future. The park is well used for dog walking, exercising, and allowing space for a neighbouring children's museum.

[1] | Staircase leading into the sliver.
[2] | The green roof, the largest in
        Connecticut, expands the site's
        existing wetland area.
[3] | The inverse-raindrop shape of the
        building also helps in reducing the
        area exposed to the sun and reduces
        the heat gain.
[4] | The sliver's stainless steel shingles
        are recyclable.

[2]

[3]

[4]

Following the natural laws of gravity, water flows across the site and within the purification plant. Gardens filter and store stormwater to prevent run-off. As the water courses toward its clean state, it creates small programme potentials within the vast space of the new park. Aligned along the base of the sliver are the finish water pumps, which distribute the clean water to the region. Landscaping, as opposed to piping, manages the stormwater drainage system.

The landscape design enlarged and augmented the existing wetlands – used as a recess point by some species of migrating birds – with indigenous species. Natural habitats were preserved in the landscape to maintain biodiversity. To achieve the environmental, functional and aesthetic objectives for the green roof, the project team selected a primary matrix of vegetation that features various species of sedum embedded across the entire roof. Roughly 7,000 flowering perennials were planted as plugs in drifts covering selected roof areas. The green roof is a low-maintenance system, and no mowing or irrigation is required. Most of the plants grow to about 15 centimetres and form full coverage within two growing seasons.

The facility's almost 3,000 square metre green roof is the largest in the state of Connecticut. It increases the project's insulation value, reduces its contribution to the urban heat-island effect, and reduces stormwater runoff. A ground-source heat-pump system, including eighty-eight wells, heats and cools the building. The system was anticipated to save 850,000 kilowatt-hours of energy each year, compared with conventional electrical-resistant heaters and air-cooled chillers. The plant's below-grade large thermal mass maintains stable temperatures and minimises the need for air conditioning. The plant's below-grade configuration also allows gravity to drive the water's movement, omitting the need for pumping during normal operation.

Building materials were selected in keeping with green design principals. The stainless steel shingles are recyclable. The terrazzo floor is made of recycled glass-chip aggregate. The cork-tile floor is made of a rapidly renewable material. Interiour finish materials were selected for their low chemical emissions. Local concrete plants were selected to provide cast-in-place and precast concrete – which makes up more than 40% of the overall building materials – thus reducing the environmental impact of the building and transportation costs. All excavated earth and land-clearing debris was salvaged and reused. Inside the sliver, all regularly occupied spaces are daylit and naturally ventilated via operable windows. All electrical lighting comes from low-energy fluorescent fixtures.

A collaborative effort with the local energy company to minimise the project's energy use resulted in significant financial subsidies and energy credits. The ground-source heating system was anticipated to generate significant annual savings for the plant and, following an incentive from the local electric utility provider, to pay for itself in three to five years.

From the beginning of the project, the design team consulted the local Connecticut Department of Environmental Protection, the US Army Corp of Engineers, and the Inland Wetland Committee to develop an extensive erosion control and plant dewatering strategy. Given the urgent need to manage and conserve water resources, this project is an example of today's best sustainable design measures and watershed management practices. Indeed, it even includes the enlargement of an existing wetland into a vibrant microenvironment that increases biodiversity.

↘ | The sliver in the surrounding landscape.

Federal
Environmental
Agency

Federal Building
Dessau, Germany
2005

Sauerbruch Hutton
Architects

Berlin, Germany

The German Federal Environmental Agency Building presents a case study for a sustainable development in the most integrated sense. Social, economical, urban, architectural, technical and material issues are being addressed in order to generate a development that not only succeeds in significantly reducing energy consumption and carbon dioxide production compared to other modern office buildings, it also makes a significant contribution to the city and provides a communicative, flexible and healthy workplace of high environmental quality.

Dessau belongs to a region that has suffered an almost complete loss of its economical basis as a consequence of the reunification of Germany. Locating the Federal Environmental Agency here is a contribution to job creation and to the establishment of new expertise in an area that – environmentally speaking – has suffered severely from its industrial past.

The location within a former industrial area demonstrates the possibilities of a brownfield site. The land has been decontaminated, and both a small existing railway station and a former gas appliance factory have been integrated into the new complex. The building's placement on this site leaves a large portion of land accessible to the public. A linear park and a permeable and enclosing structure create a spatial continuum that evokes the synergetic coexistence of nature and architecture. The large building, only ever perceptible in part, due to its sinuous shape, is well integrated into the small-scale urban context.

The main building 'snakes' to adapt to the outline of the site and to create two clear spatial zones. While the crescent of the 'Forum' invites us to use the Environmental Agency's public facilities such as the library, the auditorium, the exhibition gallery and the information centre, the more enclosed 'Atrium' constitutes the core of the institution itself. This generous circulation space, crossed by sets of bridges, provides the visual focus for surrounding offices and a communicative space for informal meetings. While the spaces around the bridgeheads provide more articulated accommodation for central facilities, the layout of the 'generic' offices around the Atrium can be varied to adapt to the ever-changing needs of the Environmental Agency.

↘ | The amoeboid concrete structure, clad in colored glass panels and wood, represents an imaginative combination of energy-saving design and technology.

| A key purpose of the use of color is to break down the potentially monolithic nature of the façade, while providing a colour code for seven different areas of the building, each of the seven sets of colour related chromatically to its neighbour.

| The more enclosed atrium provides the centre of the institution itself. The generous circulation space, crossed by sets of bridges, provides the visual focus for surrounding offices and a communicative space for informal meetings.

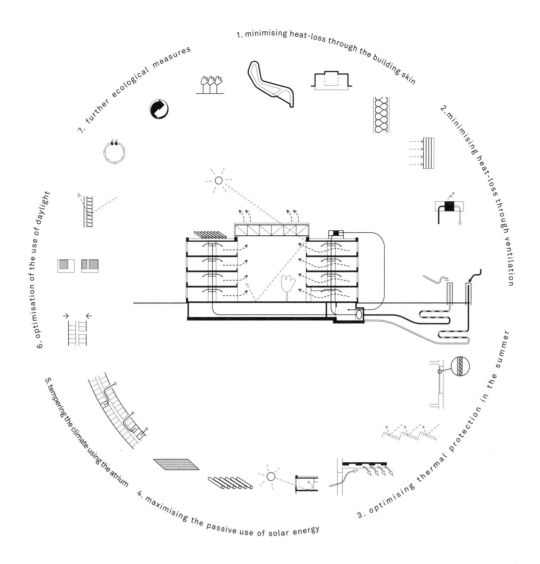

The new building combines a compact volume and a high degree of thermal insulation with strategies of intelligent engineering and the use of renewable energy sources.

The building has been designed to minimise the area of its external skin. For those offices with an external façade, very high levels of thermal wall and window insulation help to reduce heat loss. Natural ventilation and daylight penetration are maximised. The sizes of the windows have been optimised according to the specific location of each office in order to benefit from daylight without too much solar gain. Every office has an openable window, and retractable blinds provide adjustable solar shading. On days of higher or lower external temperature, a large geothermal heat exchanger enables fresh air to be conditioned naturally before it reaches the interiour spaces. The high thermal mass of the walls and ceilings and the night ventilation of the offices enable further cooling of the offices in the summer. The cooling of select areas (e.g. IT centre and kitchen) is achieved by a solar-powered adsorption chiller. Twenty per cent of the building's energy needs are met from renewable sources. Besides the geothermal and solar energy (250 square metres of photovoltaic cells have been integrated into the glazing of the Forum roof), a local landfill site provides energy for a gas turbine. All building materials were selected strictly according to their ecological and biological suitability. As part of a research programme, the performance of the building is being monitored continuously. Measurements are taken, analysed and published in order to make the experiences of this prototypical building available for the public and the profession alike.

Nearly two years after its opening, the building is starting to meet the very high original expectations in nearly all areas. Currently, in some areas, the building is using even less energy than the extremely low level originally estimated.

↘ 196 | Site plan: The building snakes in adapting to the outline of the site and to create distinct spatial inner and outer zones.

[1] | Entrance situation

[2] | While its sinuous, polychromatic features unfold intriguingly before you, its entire gestalt can be taken in only by viewing it from the air.

[1]

[2]

San Francisco Federal Building

Federal Building
San Francisco, USA
2007

Morphosis

Los Angeles, USA

The San Francisco Federal Building is a reflection of the commitment to design excellence and sustainable architecture of Morphosis and the US General Services Administration (GSA).

As part of its commitment to sustainable living, the GSA works to reduce consumption of natural resources, minimise waste, and create a healthy and productive work environment for all tenants who occupy federal workspace. The San Francisco Federal Building is a demonstration of this commitment, incorporating state-of-the art technology and performance-driven innovation.

The new federal building is a slender 20-metre-wide tower rising 18 storeys (ca. 70 m) along the northern edge of the Mission and Seventh Street site. A four-storey building annex adjoins the tower at the western edge of the site, helping to define the space that constitutes a new public plaza. In addition to this active plaza, the facility includes a number of resources that are available for public use, including a café, a childcare centre, and a conference centre.

The new Federal Building takes advantage of San Francisco's temperate climate to provide a comfortable interiour environment while reducing energy consumption.

As a whole, the building is best understood as a hybrid that includes different space-conditioning strategies appropriate for different locations in the building. The first five levels, with high concentrations of people and equipment, are fully air-conditioned. Above the fifth floor, the windows automatically adjust, allowing fresh air directly into the building for natural ventilation and free cooling. The window system creates a 'living skin' that allows the building to breathe. Breezes pass through openings on the windward side and are vented out through the leeward wall, with control based on wind speed and direction.

A computerised system, known as the building automated system (BAS), controls and monitors all of the building's mechanical equipment including the devices that are used to maintain internal environmental conditions and lighting levels. On the naturally ventilated floors, the computer system opens and closes windows, vents and sunscreens in response to temperature within the building as well as external environmental conditions. The window wall features manually operated windows so that occupants can control the internal environment and includes a heating system integrated into the mullions. During the night, the BAS opens the windows to flush out heat build-up and allows the night air to cool the building's concrete interiour. Throughout the day the thermal mass of the exposed concrete columns, shear walls and waveform ceilings help cool the occupants of the building.

| Set within a dense urban context, the San Francisco Federal Building establishes a new benchmark for the intelligent use of natural resources in the United States.

| In the tower, the design of the high-performance façades is critical to the functioning of the natural ventilation. At the southeast elevation, a perforated metal sunscreen protects the glass façade from excess solar heat gain.

[1] | Cross-section through sky garden. The slender tower rises 18 storeys.

[2] | A four-storey building annex adjoins the tower at the western edge of the site, helping to define the space that constitutes a new public plaza. In addition to this active plaza, the facility includes a number of resources that are available for public use, including a café, a childcare centre, and a conference centre.

[3] | Entrance situation

In the tower, the design of the high-performance façades is critical to the functioning of the natural ventilation. At the south-east elevation, a perforated metal sunscreen protects the glass façade from excess solar heat gain; at the north-west elevation, a series of fixed translucent sunshades are attached to an exteriour catwalk, breaking the sun's path to shade the glass.

The building is expected to surpass the General Services Administrations (GSA) energy target for heating and cooling systems. The local utility provider, PG & E, has confirmed that the project will receive an energy rebate of $250,000 on completion of construction.

Lighting is typically the largest energy cost for an office building, representing up to 40 per cent of a facility's total energy load. The new San Francisco Federal Building's lighting strategies improve the workplace and are a critical facet of this project's sustainable design. Approximately 85 per cent of the workspace is illuminated with natural light. Ambient light, the general illumination in an office, comes from sunlight channelled through the windows and reflected off walls and ceilings to extend its reach with minimum glare and intensity. With an average overall ceiling height in the tower of about 4 metres, natural daylight will penetrate deep into workspaces. Powered lights are also provided to supplement the natural light. Together, these approaches reduce energy used for lighting by approximately 26 per cent.

[1]

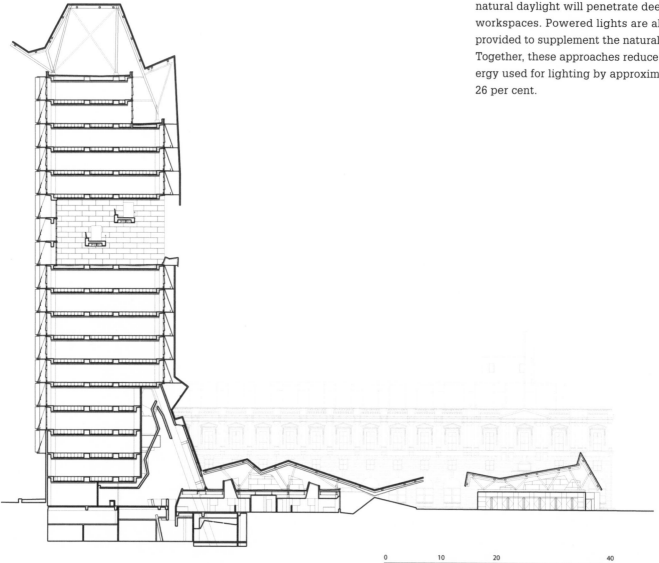

```
0        10        20              40
METERS
```

[2]

[3]

| Interiour views of the soaring entry lobby with wide, open stairs.

[1] | Lobbies and a sky garden also provide a comfortable setting for informal meetings and social interaction.

[2] | On the 11th floor, the sky garden showcases a light installation by James Turell.

[1]

[2]

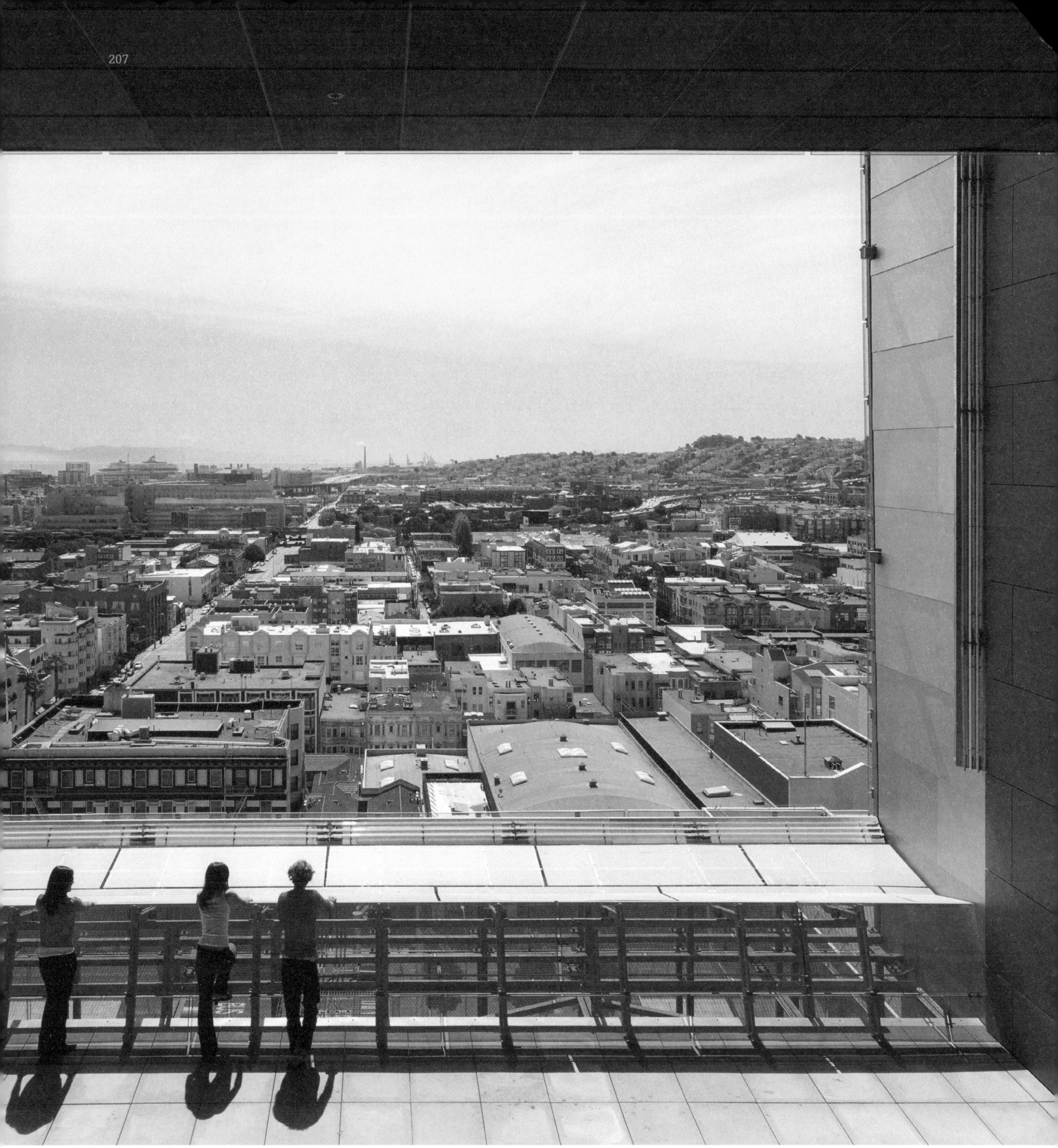

↘ | At the north-west elevation, a series
of fixed translucent sunshades are
attached to an exteriour catwalk,
breaking the sun's path.

The San Francisco Federal Building incorporates building materials and construction strategies that minimise waste and energy consumption. The building minimises pollution by replacing high proportions of Portland cement in its concrete foundations and frame. In the Federal Building's concrete mixture, 50 per cent of the pollution-intensive Portland cement is replaced with blast furnace slag, a recycled waste product from the steel industry, significantly reducing greenhouse gas emissions resulting from conventional concrete. This environmentally sound choice also results in higher-strength concrete and has a warm, light-coloured tone that contributes to the favourable daylight penetration within the office space.

The tower's high ceilings and glass façades provide 85 per cent of the building's tenants with views overlooking the city. The outer perimeter of the tower is configured with open offices and workstation partitions, maximising access to natural light. Fritted glass panels that enclose meeting rooms and offices located in the middle 'spine' of the tower, provide both privacy and access to natural light.

project

architects

INVERSAbrane

KOL/MAC LCC

Invertible Building Membrane
DuPont, USA
2005 (ongoing)

New York, USA

Current data point to buildings as the greatest source of urban pollution and energy consumption. The project recognises the significant role a building membrane can play in improving the environmental quality of both the building and the city.

The high-performance building membrane, is a project focused on going beyond the current 'green' curtain wall standard through strategic linking of advanced geometry, material and structural engineering, digital fabrication technologies and emerging expertise in ecology and biomedia.

INVERSAbrane is an exteriour membrane and infrastructure. Its performance is based on excess surface that maximises contact with the environment and creates a unique opportunity for ecosystemic exchanges between building and city. Air, water and light are recycled through it and used as sources of energy. The membrane's capacity to invert, connects exteriour and interiour into a mutually enhancing feedback system with the effect of producing greater safety and comfort for both environments.

The design of INVERSAbrane starts out with two goals. Firstly, to create a building surface that 'metabolises' air, water and sunlight through its form and material. Secondly, to increase the total surface area in order to maximise the effect.

The resulting design achieves these goals due to its complex forms and manifold surfaces based on minimal surface geometry. Scoops catch and guide water and air; exfoliation of surface increases exposure to sun and aids air filtration; and bladders store water. When INVERSAbrane cells are compared with standard façade elements of the same size, their potential to enhance the performance of the entire building's ecosystem becomes evident.

The architects believe that existing models of 'green' building envelopes are too focused on fixing the problem by adding 21st century technology to 20th century design. Therefore, their proposal takes advantage of the full range of 21st century tools both in design and production. In design, this means connecting form and performance, by combining state-of-the-art form generation with diagnostic software. In production, it involves the use of advanced materials and methods best suitable to deliver the highest quality of form and performance.

The INVERSAbrane façade system specifically targets the speculative development market and its architect-developer-end-user customer chain. To the architect, it provides a system with a vast range of non-predetermined design possibilities that he or she can steer through the proprietary interface.

To the developer, it offers immediate real-time correlations between design alternatives and cost/time/performance data. And to the end-user, it presents all the benefits of a high-performance sustainable building membrane.

[1] | Air cleaning capacity of INVERSAbrane cells based on a surface area of 1m x 1m panels.

[2] | Stills from a presentation movie depicting the application of the INVERSAbrane on the glass façade of a conventional building.

[3] | Texture variation of the INVERSAbrane.

Cell 04
Area = 1.14 m²
Air Cleaning = 441.87 m³/hr

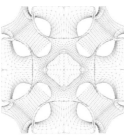

Cell 05
Area = 1.49 m²
Air Cleaning = 579.95 m³/hr

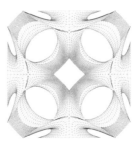

Cell 10
Area = 1.23 m²
Air Cleaning = 477.37 m³/hr

Cell 12
Area = 1.27 m²
Air Cleaning = 493.15 m³/hr

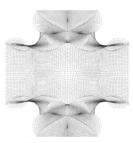

Cell 21
Area = 1.24 m²
Air Cleaning = 481.32 m³/hr

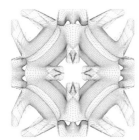

Cell 23
Area = 2.21 m²
Air Cleaning = 856.12 m³/hr

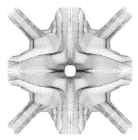

Cell 29
Area = 1.80 m²
Air Cleaning = 698.31 m³/hr

Cell 30
Area = 1.21 m²
Air Cleaning = 469.48 m³/hr

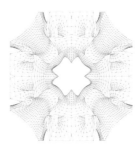

Cell 31
Area = 1.84 m²
Air Cleaning = 714.09 m³/hr

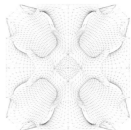

Cell 37
Area = 1.64 m²
Air Cleaning = 635.18 m³/hr

Standard Flat Exterior Cladding Panel
Area = 1 m²
Air Cleaning = 388.00 m³/hr

[1]

[2]   [3]

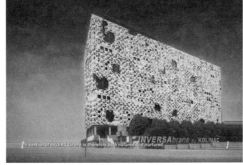

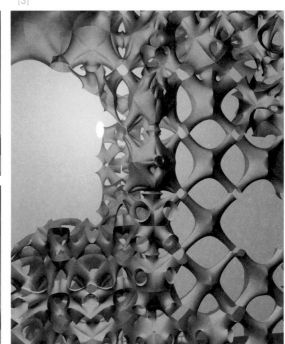

New Monte Rosa-Hut

Mountain Hut
Zermatt, Switzerland
2008 (ongoing)

Studio Monte Rosa

ETH Zurich
Zürich, Switzerland

On the edge of a glacier in pristine wilderness, the Swiss Alpine Club's (SAC) New Monte Rosa Hut is set in an extreme climatic region far from comfortable civilised supply networks. This applies to the production, the building site logistics, the autarkic infrastructure and the operation of the hut.

The project is based on a five-storey, segment-shaped wooden lathe building method. The computer-aided mechanical production process makes it possible to use traditional construction methods such as half-timber building with its geometrically complex wood junctions. The result is a wide range of possibilities for the use of timber.

The concept of the highly insulated façade is the result of a mixture of energy saving and energy production. The facet-like, metallic skin is studded with photovoltaic panels that supply the building with the necessary operational energy. A spiral-shaped glass band that follows the sun and conducts passive energy into the dining room and peripherally ascending cascade staircase is wound around the whole building and presents the guest with an impressive landscape panorama.

The Studio Monte Rosa was originally established at the Department of Architecture within the framework of the ETH Zurich's 150th anniversary for the planning and execution of the New

Monte Rosa-Hut. Students were formed into design teams, changing over a period of four semesters. The project classes comprised the planning from the conception to the provisional building project. Particular importance was attached to interdisciplinary collaboration with specialists and expert planners. The didactic concept was based on the creation of an artificial emergency situation, and the result aimed at an autarkic island solution. Following a two-year evolutionary design process, a well-known jury recommended this incisive project for implementation.

[1] | Ground floor plan
[2] | Upper floor plan

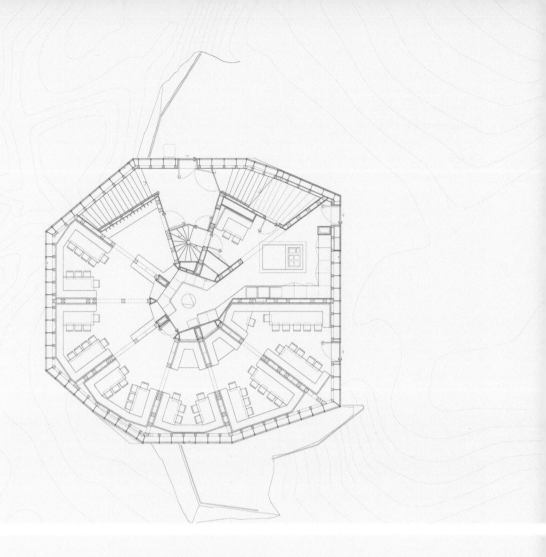

[1]

[2]

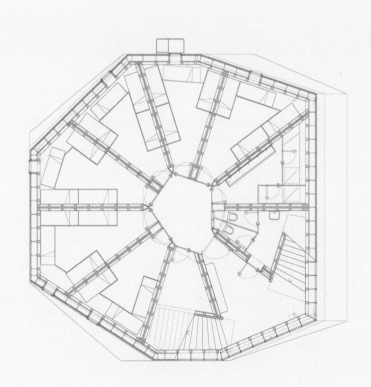

In a second stage, various chairs of the Department of Architecture and other involved departments of the ETH Zurich were formed into a research group for the research and development project.The challenge was to include knowledge of the latest technology and research in construction in the project New Monte Rosa Hut and to consolidate this knowledge. All the results of the project are orientated towards the multifaceted aspects of sustainability and are intended to be suitable for use in other projects as well.

Commencement of work on the New Monte Rosa Hut site is planned for the early summer of 2008, and the inauguration for the summer of 2009.

↘ | Model of interiour view. The four floors will be realised in a prefabricated wooden structure.

↘ | Rendered visualisation: The New
Monte Rosa-Hut is in the middle of
a natural reserve with extreme alpine
conditions.

03

Didactics
of
Engagement

This chapter discusses the work of a whole variety of organisations and individuals who have made an exemplary commitment to improving the environment we live in through their worldwide commitment to architecture and urban development. The spheres documented here range from Open Source Internet platforms to community projects in developing countries, experimental approaches to flood protection and alternative solar power stations.

Toward a Twenty-First Century Renaissance; Education, Design, and a Hopeful Human Prospect

by William A. McDonough

William McDonough is the founding principal of William McDonough + Partners, Architecture and Community Design and is known for his work in sustainability.

Each year, American colleges and universities hand out design degrees by the thousands. Credentials in hand, a veritable army of young architects and urban planners, engineers and product designers enter the job market and, with a little luck, begin to practice their professions. But what exactly is the 'system' within which they are practicing? Have their university educations prepared them to be the designers of the twenty-first century world?

These are not merely academic questions. In a very real way, designers create the human environment; they make the things we use, the places we live and work, our modes of communication and mobility. Simply put, design matters. And at a moment in our history in which the scientific community has issued serious warnings about the negative impacts of our flawed designs — from global warming and water pollution to the loss of biodiversity and natural resources — designers have a critical role to play in the creation of a more just, healthy and sustainable world.

Our colleges and universities, by and large, are not preparing design students for this crucial challenge. While design for sustainability is increasingly being seen as an important element of both foundation and specialised courses, there is still a long way to go. Consider, for example, the recent *Metropolis* magazine survey of more than 350 deans, department chairs and professors on the relevance of sustainability to design education. Though 67 per cent of respondents agreed that sustainability is relevant to their design curricula, only 14 per cent said that their schools were developing programmes to educate their teachers about sustainable design. When asked how many graduate courses their department offers that include considerations of sustainability, 28 per cent said none and 45 per cent said they did not know.

This, of course, has a profound impact on professional practice: a separate *Metropolis* survey of practising design pro-

fessionals, conducted in 2002, found that a full 70 per cent did not feel equipped to do a sustainable design job.

The impact on our world is profound as well. When architects and designers are unable to practice sustainable design, we are missing opportunities to lay the foundation for a hopeful and prosperous future. Instead of designs for buildings and products and manufacturing systems that effectively use energy and resources and generate a wealth of positive environmental, economic and social effects, we get designs that reiterate the 'take, make, and waste' sensibility of conventional industry. Instead of safe, healthy materials designed for many life cycles, we get toxic, cradle-to-grave materials designed for a one-way trip to the landfill or incinerator. In short, conventional design tends to diminish the long-term health of human culture and the natural world on which it depends.

We can do much better than this.

The first step would be to more clearly define sustainability and good design. What is it that we intend to teach young architects when we teach them about sustainable design? Typically, sustainability is used as a descriptive term for a range of cultural responses to the environmental and social impacts of economic growth. It is often defined as 'development that meets the needs of the present without compromising the ability of future generations to meet their own needs'.

Sustainable design puts that sensibility into practice. Many approaches to 'sustainable' architecture, for example, focus primarily on outlining strategies for building systems that make efficient use of energy and materials. Sustainable land planning and site design emphasises an environmentally responsive use of vegetation, water, and other natural systems. Yet, while these strategies represent a marked improvement over conventional practice, they most often rely on minimising human impact on the environment, striving only to be 'less bad.'

And 'less bad' is not good enough for our young designers. A reductive approach to design may allow architects and manufacturers to use fewer resources, produce less waste and minimise toxic emissions, but it does not change the fundamental design paradigm. As a result, many so-called 'sustainable' technologies use energy and materials within a conventional cradle-to-grave system, diluting pollution and slowing the loss of natural resources without addressing the design flaws that create waste and toxic products in the first place.

Thankfully, sustainable design is not limited to simply trying to be more efficient. A new paradigm offers a clear alternative: an ecologically intelligent framework in which the safe, regenerative productivity of nature provides models for wholly positive human designs. Within this framework, called cradle-to-cradle design, every material is designed to provide a wide spectrum of renewable assets. After a useful life as a healthy product, Cradle-to-Cradle[SM] materials (as opposed to conventional materials designed for a one-way trip from cradle-to-grave) either replenish the earth with biodegradable matter or supply high quality technical resources for the next generation of products. When materials and products are created specifically for use within these closed-loop cycles — the flow of biological materials through nature's cycles and the circulation of industrial materials from producer to customer to producer — businesses can realise both enormous short-term growth and enduring prosperity. As well, we can begin to redesign the very foundations of architecture and industry, creating systems that purify air, land and water; use current solar income and generate no toxic waste; use only safe, healthy, regenerative materials whose benefits enhance all life.

This positive agenda can redefine design education. Rather than teaching student architects and designers how to reduce the impact of their work or meet today's environmen-

tal standards, we might inspire them with an altogether different design assignment: design industrial and architectural systems for the twenty-first century that

- introduce no hazardous materials into the air, water and soil;
- measure prosperity by how much we enhance the positive effects of the human footprint;
- measure productivity by how many people are gainfully and meaningfully employed;
- measure progress by how many buildings have no smokestacks or have dangerous effluents;
- do not require regulations whose purpose is to stop us from killing ourselves too quickly;
- produce nothing that will require future generations to maintain constant vigilance;
- generate more energy than they consume;
- make every building a life-support system; and
- celebrate the abundance of biological and cultural diversity and renewable energy.

Students engaging this revolutionary design assignment need to be supported in the classroom. In the 1970s, when green architecture began to emerge in response to the energy crisis, most design students interested in creating solar-powered buildings found themselves working with faculty members who did not understand — and who did not want to understand — the principles of ecologically intelligent design. In fact, one of my professors at Yale, an architect well known for his sophisticated modernist designs, went as far as to say that 'solar energy had nothing to do with architecture'.

Vitruvius would have disagreed. The Roman master's encyclopaedic treatise on architecture, hugely influential in ancient times and again in the Renaissance, contained whole chapters on the profound significance of the sun's movement

| Fuller Theological Seminary, Pasadena, California, USA

in relation to the location of rooms, the size of apertures, thermal mass, and so on. A building insensitive to the movement of the sun would have left Vitruvius aghast.

But not the modernists. Indeed, my professor's rebuttal suggests just how far the modernist project had divorced architecture from place and from the past. Following Le Corbusier, the modernist ideal was 'one single building for all nations and climates'. The house was to be 'a machine for living in'. No need to understand local energy flows in that paradigm; just add fossil fuels. Style, too, was fiercely ideological, defined by the Bauhaus maxim 'less is more'. Energetically applied, the 'less is more' lens had a clarifying effect on architectural theory and practice, but as it calcified into academic rhetoric, its effect in the classroom was ultimately chilling.

And so architecture students, their ideas dismissed by their teachers, often graduated and began to practice ecological design without a suitable aesthetic foundation. The results were less than handsome. Architects who designed solar-powered buildings typically delivered machines for living in with solar collectors on the roof. They were crude and utilitarian and they did not really change the basic modernist paradigm. Same materials, same generally insensitive relation to place and history, same ecological illiteracy.

The architecture critic Nicholas Pevsner wrote 'a bicycle shed is a building; a cathedral is architecture'. The new solar buildings in the 1970s were seen as bicycle sheds, and, in fact, this is what they were. This cast a shadow over ecological design for years, which meant that our universities were not blessed with a new generation of faculty members capable of helping students pursue aesthetically rich designs that also expressed ecological intelligence.

That has begun to change. It is worth noting that even though only 14 per cent of the design educators responding

to the *Metropolis* survey said that their schools were developing sustainable design curricula for instructors, 67 per cent did see the relevance of sustainability to design education. Even ten years ago that number would have been considerably smaller.

Moreover, the work of prominent architects is now demonstrating that ecological design and aesthetic excellence create a wonderful synergy. Consider Norman Foster's designs for the Reichstag and the Commerzbank Tower in Germany and London's new City Hall, all of which combine a formally rich design sensibility with a keen sensitivity to the larger ecological context of architecture. As *The New York Times* has reported, Foster is 'mining the expressive potential of low-energy construction' to create buildings 'as elegant as any in the world'.

In the Commerzbank Tower, Foster created a 60-storey atrium down the centre of the building and built multi-storey sky gardens, replacing air conditioning with natural ventilation. The Reichstag's domed assembly hall is also naturally ventilated and its three-storey shade follows the revolution of the sun. The spherical shape of London's City Hall reduces solar gain, so the building is kept cool using far less energy. As described in *The Times*, it should put to rest any lingering notion that an ecologically intelligent building is destined to be a bicycle shed:

'In the gorgeous Assembly chamber, an oculus of unusually transparent water-white glass (regular glass has a slightly greenish tint) opens the chamber northward through a diagonal fretwork of tubular steel supports to a splendid vista of the Tower of London and London Bridge. The room is bathed in light as limpid and serene as a Vermeer painting (this is also is also part of the low energy scheme: the Assembly need only switch on the lights for night-time and televised events.)'

| Adam Joseph Lewis Center for
Environmental Studies, Oberlin College,
Oberlin, Ohio, USA, 2001

Now, when a student expresses interest in ecological design, not only is there no reasonable argument for dismissing his or her enthusiasm, there are inspiring examples in the world he or she can emulate.

This is a salutary change in the general atmosphere of design education, but it is not enough to power a true transformation. The creativity unleashed by our new design assignment – which is really a lifetime design assignment – can only be sustained in the classroom when the classroom itself embodies the same values. As the educator David Orr has pointed out, architecture always serves a pedagogical function; the design of buildings teaches and reinforces how we use resources, how we relate to nature and what our culture values. It is absurd, he believes, to teach young people about the world, especially young people interested in intelligently redesigning the world, in buildings that devour fossil fuels, have no relation to their surroundings, are generally uncomfortable and uninspiring, and express ignorance of how nature works.

To address the shortcomings of the contemporary classroom, Orr worked with William McDonough + Partners to design an educational facility, The Adam Joseph Lewis Center for Environmental Studies, that teaches ecological intelligence rather than ecological illiteracy. The result: a building that restores the local landscape, accrues solar income, filters water, creates habitat for living things and, as Orr writes, offers students, 'the kind of education that prepares people for lives and livelihoods suited to a planet with a biosphere that operates by the laws of ecology and thermodynamics'.

Drawing the majority of its power from solar energy, the Lewis Center already has exceedingly low energy demands, and with the addition of more solar panels to the site, it may one day produce more energy than it needs to operate. Its

other sustainable design features include geothermal wells for heating and cooling; daylighting and fresh air delivery throughout; an extended botanical garden that recovers nutrients from circulating water on-site; and a landscape that offers social gathering spaces, instructional gardens and orchards, and a newly planted grove of native trees, which has begun the process of re-establishing the habitat of the building's northern Ohio location.

The building and its classrooms have become the centre of a learning community. The comfortable, sunlit classrooms and public gathering areas encourage mingling, communication and reflection. Inside and out, the building provides opportunities for learning how nature and human industry can work together – the foundation of ecological literacy.

Perhaps the most moving lesson the building imparts is that the human presence in the landscape can be regenerative. Not simply benign or less bad, but positive, vital and good. This is not a rhetorical lesson. At Oberlin, habits of mind grow out of daily interactions with wind, water, soil and trees as well as the workings of experimental building and energy systems; they become the skills and knowledge that inform intelligent design.

Learning such as this can be integrated into the curricula of many disciplines. Chemists aware of the concerns of sustainability can master the skills necessary to assess the environmental health and safety of industrial and architectural materials. 'Green' engineers, who are employed throughout the sustainable design process, can garner the technical know-how to develop an array of sustainable systems, from solar collection technology to chemical recycling processes that allow the reuse of valuable materials. MBA (Master of Business Administration) degrees that understand the value of design for the triple top line – the creation of ecological, economic and social value through

cradle-to-cradle product development – will generate extraordinary value for shareholders. As our educational institutions recognise this new kind of literacy, they would provide a great benefit to students with revamped curricula that reflect the interdisciplinary values of a sustainable world.

When young professionals schooled in good sustainable design begin to practise, they can change the nature of 'the possible'. Ten years ago, if a young architect walked into a firm and said, 'I think we can build a green roof', he or she would have met considerable resistance – there was not a single green roof in North America at the time. Now, however, thousands of architects have seen the multiple successful examples that have not only met budget and time restrictions but have created a new way of thinking about the relationship between building and landscape. At Ford Motor Company's new River Rouge manufacturing facility, for example, a four-hectare green roof that effectively filters stormwater runoff was built with first-cost savings of $10 million. When a young architect suggests a green roof today, his or her superiors know that some of the smartest firms are creating successful, cost-effective projects.

Imagine a 21st century world in which our colleges and universities prepare students for lives and livelihoods that reimagine the possible. The very purpose and nature of learning would evolve from what is largely a celebration of human intelligence towards a new sensibility that seeks to replace dominion over nature with a more fulfilling relationship between humanity and the natural world. This movement away from simple stewardship, and toward a sense of kinship with life – what the biologist E. O. Wilson calls biophilia – is a source of creativity and deep learning. If this century is to be known for prosperity, beauty, and the restoration of our world, understanding our kinship with nature needs to become one of the foundations of cultural life. Architecture and design, with their profound ability to create new relationships between people and their world, is uniquely positioned to engender such a change. Our educational institutions, inasmuch as they support and nurture this new literacy, can be home to the flowering of a twenty-first century renaissance.

Green Design

by Ken Yeang

Ken Yeang is the prinicipal of the UK based architecture practice Llewelyn Davis Yeang and author of the seminal book „Ecodesign. Instruction Manual for Ecological Design".

Our work on green design, although it shares the same aims as many other green designers, is quite different. The main differentiation is that it starts from the ecological perspective, as an ecologist.

The *need to* save our environment for future generations is one of the greatest challenges that humankind must address today; this task is fuelled by the growing realisation that if we maintain our current rate of growth and consumption, this may be our last millennium on Earth. Therefore the compelling question for any designer is: how do we design for a sustainable future?

Just as much as this question concerns the design professions, it is also a question that concerns industry; many corporations now anxiously seek to understand the environmental consequences of their current activities and attempt to envision what their impact might be if their business were sustainable. The most committed businesses must seek ways to realise their vision through ecologically benign strategies, new business models, production systems, materials and processes. An ecologically responsive built environment will undoubtedly change the way we work and will significantly impact the ecologically profligate way of life pursued by many of us in developed and developing countries.

The most effective ecological approach to business practice, as well as design, will develop through environmental integration. If we integrate everything we do or make in our built environment (which, by definition, consists of our buildings, facilities, infrastructure, products, refrigerators, toys, etc.) with the natural environment in a seamless and benign way, there will be no detrimental environmental impact whatsoever. Simply stated, ecodesign is design for bio-integration; this can be regarded as having three facets: physical, systemic and temporal. Addressing each of these facets successfully is, of course, easier said than done; but herein lies our challenge as designers.

We can start by looking at nature. Nature without humans exists in stasis. Can our businesses and our built environment imitate nature's processes, structures and functions? Ecosystems have no waste; everything is recycled within the system. Thus by imitating the ecosystem, our built environment should produce no waste; all emissions and products would be continuously reused or recycled and eventually reintegrated with the natural environment. Designing to imitate ecosystems is ecomimesis. This is the fundamental premise for ecodesign: our built environment must imitate ecosystems in all respects.

Nature regards humans as just one of its many species. What differentiates humans from other natural organisms is their capability to force large-scale devastating change on the environment. Such changes are often the consequence of rapacious (manufacturing, construction) or superficially benign (recreation and transport) activities.

Our built forms are essentially enclosures erected to protect us from inclement weather and to enable activities (whether residential, office, manufacturing, warehousing, etc.) to take place. Ecologically, a building is just a high concentration of materials extracted and manufactured, often using non-renewable energy resources, from some distant place in the biosphere and transported to a particular location and assembled into a built form or an infrastructure (road, bridge, sewer, etc.) whose subsequent operations create further environmental consequences and whose eventual afterlife must also be accommodated.

There is a great deal of confusion and misperception as to what exactly constitutes ecological design. It is easy to be misled or seduced by technology and to think that if we assemble enough eco-gadgetry such as solar collectors, photovoltaic cells, biological recycling systems, building automation systems and double-skin façades in one single building that this can automatically be considered ecological architecture. Although these technologies are commendable applications of low energy systems they are merely useful components leading towards ecological architecture; they represent some of the means of achieving an ecological end product. Ecological design is not just about low-energy systems; to be fully effective these technologies need to be thoroughly integrated into the building fabric; they will also be influenced by the physical and climatic conditions of the site. The nature of the problem is therefore site-specific; there will never be a standard 'one size fits all' solution.

The other misperception is that if a building achieves a high score on a green rating scale then all is well. Of course, nothing could be further from the truth; this attitude can engender self-complacency, whereupon no further action is taken to improve environmental degradation. Green rating systems are useful in publicising certain goals, however, they should be considered as threshold standards that designers should aim at achieving and exceeding.

In a nutshell, ecodesign should be viewed as the design of the built environment as just one system within the natural environment. The system's existence has ecological consequences; the way it functions and interacts with other systems over its entire life cycle must be benignly integrated with the natural environment. In this way it is the life cycle analysis of the system, rather than its value at any one particular point in time, that gives a better idea of its cumulative effect on its neighbouring systems.

Ecosystems are definable units in a biosphere; as such they should contain both biotic (living) and abiotic (non-life-supporting) constituents acting together as a whole. Following this model, our businesses and our built environment should be designed analogously to the ecosystem's physical content, composition and processes. For instance, besides regarding buildings as we do currently, as artistic endeavours or as serviced enclosures, we should regard them as artefacts that need to be operationally integrated with nature. It should be self-evident that the material composition of our built environment is almost entirely inorganic, whereas ecosystems contain a complement of both biotic and abiotic constituents, i.e. organic and inorganic components.

The enormous number of existing buildings, as well as our current manufacturing and processing activities, are making the biosphere more and more inorganic and increasingly simplified biologically. To continue doing what we have always done without balancing the abiotic with the biotic content means simply adding to the biosphere's artificiality, thereby making it increasingly inorganic and reducing its complexity and diversity. We must first reverse this trend by starting to balance our built environment with greater levels of biomass; by ameliorating biodiversity and ecological connectivity in the built forms and by complementing their inorganic content with appropriate organic biomass.

We should improve the ecological linkages between our activities, be they design or business processes, with the surrounding landscape in ways that connect them both horizontally and vertically. Achieving these linkages ensures a wider level of species connectivity, interaction, mobility and sharing of resources across boundaries. Such real improvements in connectivity enhance biodiversity and further increase habitat resilience and species survival. An obvious demonstration of horizontal connectivity is the provision of ecological corridors and linkages in regional planning which are crucial in making urban patterns more biologically viable. Besides improved horizontal connectivity, vertical connectivity within the built form is also necessary since most buildings are not single storey but multi-storey. Design must extend ecological linkages vertically from the foundations to the rooftops.

More important than the enhancement of ecological linkages is the biological integration of the inorganic products inherent in the built environment with the landscape so that the two become mutually ecosystemic. In this way we can create 'human-made ecosystems' compatible with nature's ecosystems and by doing so we will enhance the ability of human-made ecosystems to sustain life in the biosphere.

Ecodesign is also about the discernment of the ecology of the site; any design or business activity should take place with the objective of integrating benignly with an ecosystem. In the case of site planning we must first understand the properties of the locality's ecosystem before imposing any intended human activity upon it. Every site has an ecology with a limited capacity to withstand the stresses imposed upon it; if stressed beyond this capacity the ecology will be damaged irrevocably. Stress can be caused just as much by minimal localised impact (such as the clearing of a small land area for access) as by the total devastation of the entire landscape (such as the clearing of all trees and vegetation, levelling the topography and the diversion of existing waterways).

In order to identify the capacity of a site to withstand human intervention, an analysis of the existing ecology should be carried out. We must ascertain, for example, the structure of the site's ecosystems, energy flow and species diversity. Then we must identify which parts of the site, if any, have different ecosystems and which parts are particularly sensitive. Finally, we must consider the likely impact of the intended construction and use. This is, of course, a major undertaking, however it needs to be done to better understand and appreciate the nature of a site. To be thorough and effective, this type of detailed analysis should be carried out diurnally and seasonally over a period of a year or more. To reduce this lengthy process, landscape architects have developed the 'layer-cake' method; this sieve mapping technique enables designers to map the landscape as a series of separate layers that provide a simplified matrix for the investigation of a site's ecology.

As the layers are mapped, they can be overlaid and the interaction of the layers can be evaluated in relation to the proposed land use. The final product of this study is a composite map that can be used to guide the proposed site planning (e.g. the disposition of the access roads, water management, drainage patterns and shaping of the built forms). It is important to understand that the sieve mapping method generally treats the site's ecosystems statically and may ignore the dynamic forces taking place between the layers within an ecosystem. As mentioned above, the separation of the layers is a convenient intellectual construct that simplifies the complex natural interactions between layers. Therefore, the comprehensive analysis of an ecosystem requires more than sieve mapping – the interlayer relationships should also be examined.

As designers, we should also look into ways of configuring built forms, the operational systems for our built environment and our businesses as low-energy systems. In addressing these systems we need to look into ways of improving the internal comfort conditions of our buildings. There are essentially five ways of doing this: Passive Mode, Mixed Mode, Full Mode, Productive Mode and Composite Mode, the latter being a composite of all the preceding modes.

The practise of sustainable design requires that we look first at Passive Mode (or bioclimatic) design strategies, then we can move on to Mixed Mode, Full Mode, Productive Mode and Composite Mode, all the while adopting progressive strategies to improve comfort conditions relative to external conditions.

Meeting contemporary expectations for office environment comfort conditions cannot generally be achieved by Passive Mode or by Mixed Mode alone. The internal environment often needs to be supplemented by the use of external sources of energy, as in Full Mode. Full Mode uses electro-mechanical systems often powered by external energy sources – whether from fossil-fuel derived sources or from local ambient sources such as wind or solar power.

Passive Mode means designing for improved internal comfort conditions over external conditions without the use of any electro-mechanical systems. Examples of Passive Mode strategies include the adoption of suitable building orientation and configuration in relation to the local climate as well as the selection of appropriate building materials. When considering the design of the façade issues of solid-to-glazed area ratios, thermal insulation values, the incorporation of natural ventilation and the use of vegetation are also important.

Building design strategy must start with Passive Mode or bioclimatic design, as this can significantly influence the configuration of the built form and its enclosure systems. Passive Mode requires an understanding of the climatic conditions of the locality; the designer should not merely synchronise the building design with the local meteorological conditions, but optimise the ambient energy of the locality to create improved internal comfort conditions without the use of any electro-mechanical systems. The fundamental nature of these decisions clearly dictates that once the building configuration, orientation and enclosure are considered, the further refinement of a design should lead to the adoption of choices that will enhance its energy efficiency. If, as an alternative, a design solution is developed that has not previously optimised the Passive Mode options, then these non-energy efficient design decisions will need to be corrected by supplementary Full Mode systems. Such a remedy would make nonsense of low-energy design. Furthermore if the design optimises a building's Passive Modes, it remains at an improved level of comfort during any electrical power failure. If the Passive Modes have not been optimised, then whenever there is no electricity or external energy source the building may become intolerable to occupy.

Mixed Mode buildings use some electro-mechanical systems such as ceiling fans, double façades, flue atriums and evaporative cooling.

Full Mode relies entirely on the use of electro-mechanical systems to create suitable internal comfort conditions. This is the option chosen for most conventional buildings. If clients and users insist on having consistent comfort conditions throughout the year, the result will inevitably lead to Full Mode design. It must be clear now that low-energy design is essentially a user-driven condition and a lifestyle issue. We must appreciate that Passive Mode and Mixed Mode design can never compete with the comfort levels of the high-energy, Full Mode conditions.

Productive Mode is where a building generates its own energy. Common examples of this today can be seen in the generation of electricity through the use of photovoltaic panels that are powered by solar power and wind turbines that harness wind energy. Ecosystems use solar energy that is transformed into chemical energy by the photosynthesis of green plants, which in turn drives the ecological cycle. If ecodesign is to be ecomimetic, we should seek to do the same, however we will need to do so on a much larger scale.

The inclusion of systems that create Productive Modes inevitably leads to sophisticated technological systems that in turn increase the use of material resources, the inorganic content of the built form, the embodied energy content and the attendant impact on the environment.

Composite Mode is a combination of all the above modes in proportions that vary over the seasons of the year.

Ecodesign also requires the designer to use materials and assemblies that facilitate reuse, recycling and their eventual reintegration with ecological systems. Here again, we need to be ecomimetic in our use of materials in the built environment: in ecosystems, all living organisms feed on continual flows of matter and energy from their environment to stay alive, and all living organisms continually produce 'waste'. However ecosystems do not actually generate waste since one species' waste is really another species' food. Thus, matter cycles continually through the web of life. To be truly ecomimetic, the materials we produce should also take their place within the closed loop where waste becomes food.

Currently we regard everything produced by humans as eventual rubbish or waste material that is either burned or ends up in landfill sites. The new question for designers, manufacturers and businesses is: how can we use this waste material? If our materials are readily biodegradable, they can return into the environment through decomposition. If we want to be ecomimetic, we should think, at the very early design stages, about how a building, its components and its outputs can be reused and recycled. These design considerations will determine the materials to be used, the ways in which the building fabric is to be assembled, how the building can be adapted over time and how the materials can be reused after the building has reached the limits of its useful life.

If we consider the last point, reuse, in a little more detail, we come to an increasingly important conclusion. To facilitate the reuse of, let us say, a structural component, the connection between the components should be a mechanical, i.e. bolted rather than welded so that the joint can be released easily. If, in addition to being easily demountable, the components were modular, then the structure could be easily demounted and reassembled elsewhere. This leads to the concept of design for disassembly (DfD), which has its roots in sustainable design.

Another major design issue is the systemic integration of our built forms, operational systems and internal processes with the natural ecosystems that surround us. Such integra-

tion is crucial because without it these systems will remain disparate artificial items that could be potential pollutants. Unfortunately many of today's buildings only achieve eventual integration through biodegradation that requires a long-term process of natural decomposition.

While manufacture and design for recycling and reuse relieves the problem of deposition of waste, we should integrate both organic waste (e.g. sewage, rainwater runoff, wastewater, food wastes, etc.) and inorganic waste.

There is a very appropriate analogy between ecodesign and surgical prosthetics. Ecodesign is essentially design that integrates human-made systems both mechanically and organically with the natural host system – the ecosystem. A surgical prosthetic device also has to integrate with its organic host being – the human body. Failure to integrate will result in dislocation in both cases. These are the exemplars of what our buildings and our businesses should achieve: the total physical, systemic and temporal integration of our human-made, built environment with our organic host in a benign and positive way. There are, of course, a large number of theoretical and technical problems to be solved before we have a truly ecological built environment, however, we should draw encouragement from the fact that our intellect has allowed us to create prosthetic organs that can integrate with the human body. The next challenge will be to integrate our buildings, our cities and all human activities with the natural ecosystems that surround us.

Projects

20K $ House

Low Income House
Alabama, USA
2005 (ongoing)

Rural Studio

Auburn University, School of Architecture
Auburn, USA

Rural Studio, an architecture programme within the School of Architecture at Auburn University is in its fourteenth academic year and has designed and built more than fifty community projects and charity homes in West Alabama and educated more than four hundred architecture students in a service-learning model that has garnered national and international recognition.

The HERO Housing Resource Center (HRC), a local Hale County non-profit organisation, asked Rural Studio to become a partner to bridge current barriers in accessing affordable federal housing programs. The region is plagued by poverty: according to the Alabama Departement of Economic and Community Affairs, roughly one-third of this region's residents live below the poverty level, with only 59 per cent of the US per capita income. More than one-quarter of the population is currently receiving food stamps, and the percentage of the residents who are unemployed, at 13.1 per cent, more than doubles the average for the state of Alabama.

The overall goal of the $20,000 (20K) house is to design and develop a range of home plans and prototypes that can be built by local contractors under the United States Department of Agriculture's Rural Housing Service Section 502 Guaranteed Rural Housing Loan Program for construction and homeowner financing. This means that the total cost of materials and labour should be no more than $20,000. The idea of the 20K house is to provide housing for a single, low-income individual for a mortgage of $20,000, which comes to a monthly payment of about $64 per month. This creates an opportunity to provide an alternative to the trailer home.

As a possible prototype for a replicable home, it is designed to be built by a contractor, with standard shop materials. The prototype could ultimately be produced rapidly by a general contractor, in turn providing labour and stimulating the local economy.

↘ | Front elevation. The design for the house is not client or site specific, but rather intended as a prototype for low-income housing.

The building is a traditional wood framed structure, erected upon a platform frame. The exterior is entirely clad with corrugated tin, to provide a simple but durable aesthetic. A generous front porch provides a buffer space to the entrance of the building, allowing for a social public interface to the street, and ample protection from the elements. The interiour space is very open, with very few partitions. The total interiour area amounts to roughly 40 square metres. The walls and ceiling are clad with sheetrock. By opening up the space and providing a three-metre-high ceiling, this allows for the room to feel very open. There is direct and unobstructed circulation, creating a situation throughout where all the service electrical, plumbing and storage can be localised in one wall.

The scale and tightness of the interiour space also provides for good ventilation, reducing the need for mechanical cooling and also allows for relatively low heating costs. A screened porch is provided on the rear of the building. This adds an additional room to the house, which can be used for much of the year in Alabama's temperate climate. This also allows for the possibility of an additional interiour room.

[1] | Floor plan. The interiour space is vastly open, with very few partitions.

[2] | Longitudinal section.

[3] | Side elevation. The walls and ceiling are clad with sheetrock. A screen porch is provided on the rear of the building, which adds an additional room to the house.

[4] | Interiour view. The total interiour space amounts to approximately 40 square metres.

[1]

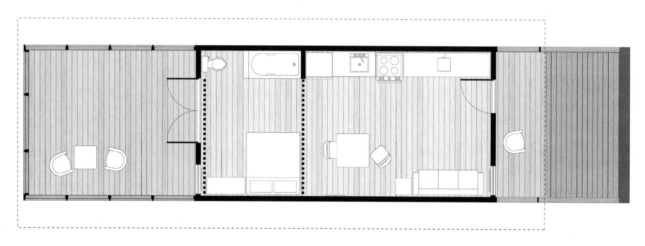

[2]

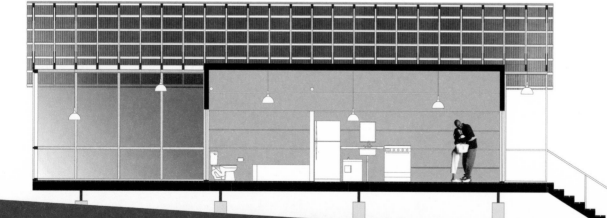

[3]

[4]

Kikoo Water Project

Water Distribution System
Kikoo, Cameroon
2007 (ongoing)

Engineers Without Borders

Yale Student Chapter
New Haven, USA

Engineers Without Borders is a non-profit humanitarian organisation established to partner with developing communities worldwide in order to improve their quality of life. This partnership involves the implementation of sustainable engineering projects, while involving and training internationally responsible engineers and engineering students.

The Yale Chapter of Engineers Without Borders is an undergraduate humanitarian organisation. The group is made up of students heralding a variety of backgrounds, with dedicated professional mentors and faculty advisors.

Clean water has been the focus of the group since it began three years ago. Over one billion people lack access to clean water throughout the world and approximately two million children die each year from diarrhoea. This could be prevented with access to a clean source of drinking water.

The community of Kikoo, Cameroon has historically collected water from polluted streams. These sources are exposed to contamination because they lie at the bottom of large valleys, and are unprotected from the animal grazing, bathing and the washing of clothes that occurs in the watershed. During the dry season, some families boil their water to purify it. However, this uses fuel wood, which is not abundant in the area. During the rainy season, some people manage to

collect rainwater from roofs as domestic water. Neither of these provides a sustainable solution to the lack of clean water within the community.

Sustainability is a key aspect throughout the entirety of the design process of the Kikoo Water Project. The group incorporates the community into the project as much as possible, and collaborate with their on-site contact continuously to ensure that the community members feel not only involved, but develop a sense of ownership of their water system. Local materials and construction practices are integrated into the implementation of the design. The goal of the project is to provide a source of clean drinking water for the community without disturbing the local surroundings, both social and environmental. This ensures that the solution will provide clean water for the community indefinitely.

↘ 236 | Excavating the storage tank site
↘ 237 | In only two weeks, five Yale students,
four professional engineers and
two Cameroonian students made
significant progress on the water
distribution system they had designed
over the course of one year.

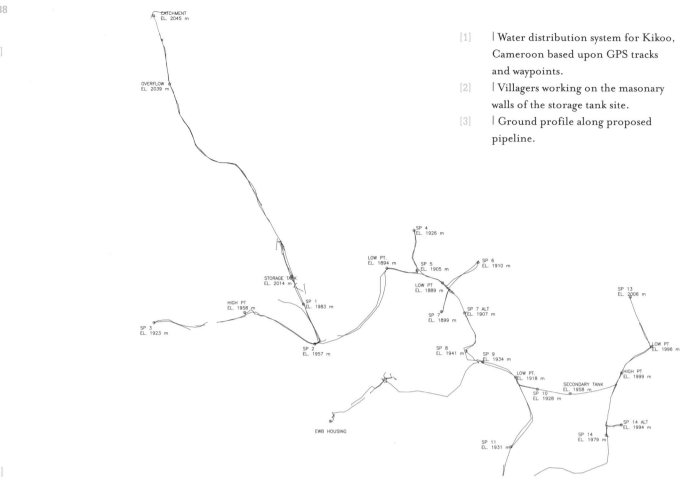

CATCHMENT
EL. 2045 m

OVERFLOW
EL. 2039 m

SP 4
EL. 1926 m

LOW PT.
EL. 1894 m

SP 5
EL. 1905 m

SP 6
EL. 1910 m

STORAGE TANK
EL. 2014 m

LOW PT
EL. 1889 m

SP 13
EL. 2006 m

SP 1
EL. 1983 m

HIGH PT
EL. 1958 m

SP 7
EL. 1899 m

SP 7 ALT
EL. 1907 m

SP 3
EL. 1923 m

LOW PT.
EL. 1996 m

SP 2
EL. 1957 m

SP 8
EL. 1941 m

SP 9
EL. 1934 m

LOW PT.
EL. 1918 m

SECONDARY TANK
EL. 1958 m

HIGH PT
EL. 1999 m

SP 10
EL. 1928 m

EWB HOUSING

SP 14 ALT
EL. 1994 m

SP 14
EL. 1979 m

SP 11
EL. 1931 m

[1] | Water distribution system for Kikoo, Cameroon based upon GPS tracks and waypoints.

[2] | Villagers working on the masonary walls of the storage tank site.

[3] | Ground profile along proposed pipeline.

[1]

[2]

[3]

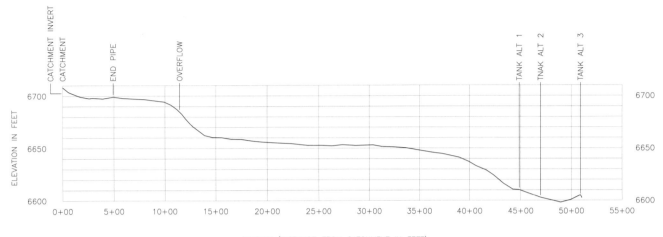

The proposed solution is a gravity-fed water distribution system. An uncontaminated artesian spring has been located, which will provide the source of the community's drinking water. The system will feature a sealed spring water catchment box that will ensure that the source of clean water is kept both sustainable and uncontaminated. The water will travel from the catchment box to an overflow tank, which has been included in the design in order to avoid backpressure behind the catchment box, as well as to provide a suitable location to discharge high seasonal flows.

The overflow tank is ideally located in order to utilise the excess water for agricultural irrigation, as well as to avoid erosion of the surrounding landscape. The water will then be piped to an 18,000-litre storage tank, which will provide the community with a consistent flow during times of peak demand. A network of pipes will distribute the water to fourteen public standpipes throughout the community.

Approximately seven kilometres of pipes will be needed to reach the entire community.

When designing the various components of the water distribution system, care was taken to not revert to old designs that had already been used for similar applications in the past. Every design is an opportunity to improve on and innovate past ideas. Every situation and problem encountered is unique, and requires special consideration and creativity. The overflow and storage tanks each feature a unique drainage system, consisting of a sloped base that directs water into a convenient floor drain.

It is important that the system can be easily cleaned and maintained in order to ensure that the water remains uncontaminated. Each valve was carefully considered and serves a specific purpose, whether it is to allow the water to circumvent a certain portion of the system or to allow the community to sample water from a specific location

in the system. The hydraulics of the system were carefully analysed in order to make sure the water pressure in the system would never be so great as to burst the piping, but would provide sufficient power in order to reach as much of the community as possible.

Another goal of the project is to provide valuable hands-on experience for the students. It is important for the undergraduates to attain an international sense of social responsibility, as well as to gain an appreciation for engineering outside of the classroom. For young engineers to become enthusiastic and excited about the engineering profession, while creating real change around the world, is an invaluable experience.

Living Tebogo

Home for Handicapped Children
Johannesburg, South Africa
2005

BASEhabitat

University of Art
Linz, Austria

[1] | Site plan. The surrounding area is dominated largely by self-made buildings and shacks.

[2] | Elevation of kitchen and dining building

[3] | Elevation of therapy building

Orange Farm is a township in the south-west of Johannesburg. The social situation is characterised by poverty, AIDS and unemployment. The appearance of the development is largely dominated by buildings or shacks made mostly of sheet metal, corrugated iron or parts of cars. In summer it can become unbearably hot in these shacks (up to 45°C), while during winter nights it can be noticeably cold (down to 2°C).

The BASEhabitat Group of the University of Linz was commissioned by the Tebogo Home for Handicapped Children. The Austrian NGO SARCH established this contact. The home for almost fifty children had become too small. In a group of twenty-five students, BASEhabitat planned and built a dining hall with a new kitchen, as well as a therapy building with sanitary facilities. A generously dimensioned pergola (covered garden walkway) connects the buildings to each other. The buildings erected in Tebogo maintain an agreeable indoor climate throughout the year – without the use of energy. In this way, fluctuations in temperature have been reduced to only 9°C. Local workers, especially women, were integrated into the project.

The building materials (concrete blocks, earth, clay, straw, timber and grass mats) were acquired directly from the township in order to strengthen the local economy and to make repetition simpler at a later date. One of the main aims was to make buildings that suited the needs of the children. They received a home that conveyed a sense of security and the enjoyment of life.

Conventional living spaces in South Africa are subjected to extreme fluctuations in temperature. In Johannesburg (around 2,000 m above sea level) winter temperatures fall to -1°C. Temperatures in habitations in the townships fall as low as 3 to 6°C in winter, and highs of 45°C in summer. In winter, low temperatures need to be counteracted, particularly in the homes of ill or disabled persons. This is usually managed by electrical heating – an ecologically extremely questionable method that is almost never affordable for the inhabitants. Pleasant and comfortable indoor temperatures are rarely attained, neither in summer nor in winter.

[1]

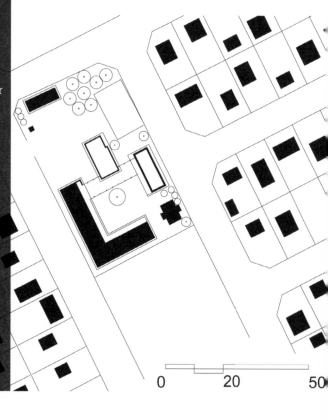

0   20   50

[2]

[3]

The Living Tebogo project had the declared goal of attaining a comfortable minimum of 18°C in winter and maximum of 29°C in summer – without the use of 'external' energies or mechanical heating or cooling, but only via building and planning measures and decisions. Research data drawn from climate studies, computer-animated design models and from experience were collected to form the basis for the design of the Tebogo Home for the Disabled. The group achieved its self-set goals when the buildings were constructed.

This result has an exemplary quality and could, in principle, be repeated all over Africa. It should be noted that any traditional construction method in these areas is much more effective at achieving such positive results than any 'modern' building technology or any of the housing structures in the townships inhabited by the poor.

Essentially, through the use of cost-free materials like clay and grass, that are available to all, and through the integration of local workers, the Tebogo project demonstrates a way towards the economically and ecologically sustainable management of the global climate issue via construction projects.

| Floor plan. BASEhabitat planned and built a dining building with a new kitchen and a therapy building with sanitary facilities. A generously dimensioned pergola, a garden hall, connects the buildings with each other.

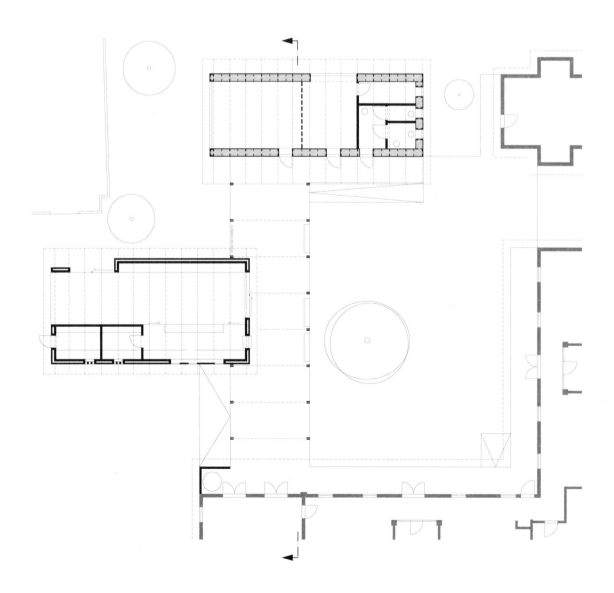

[1] | Climate concept winter. Heating
        with the sun.
[2] | Climate concept summer. Cooling
        with the construction.
[3] | Elevation of the therapy building
        made mainly from earth, clay, straw,
        timber and grass mats.

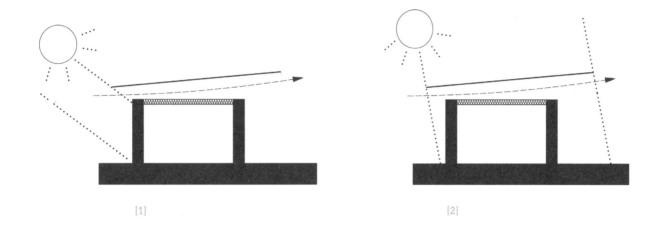

[1]   [2]

[3]

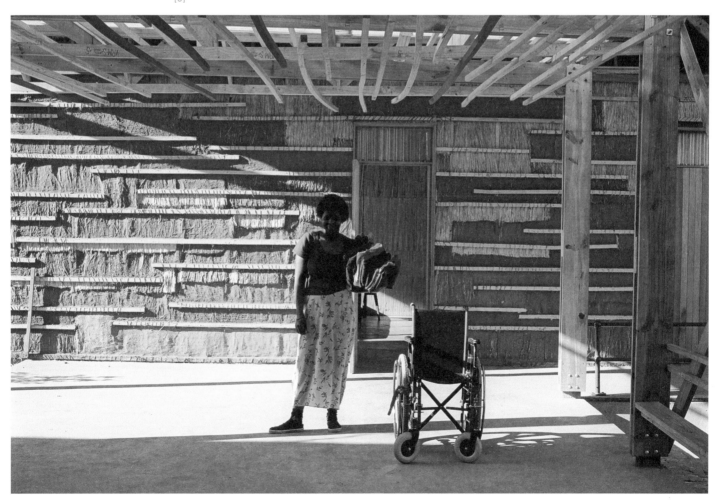

Schulbausteine für Gando e.V.

School Building
Gando, Burkina Faso
2005 (ongoing)

Diébédo Francis Kéré

Gando, Burkina Faso
Berlin, Germany

The project site is in the 2,500-people village Gando, in Burkina Faso in the West African Sahel. Like many villages in West Africa, Gando suffers from underdevelopment. The people born there stand little chance of accessing either education or development. The illiteracy rate in the village lies well above the national average of 87 per cent. In order to develop economically and continue to exist as a community, the village urgently requires support for education.

By building a school in cooperation with the whole village community, Schulbausteine für Gando e.V. has created a level of enthusiasm and optimism that never existed in the village before. Because the initiator grew up in this village, people see education as a great opportunity for their children.

It all began with a request from the villagers to one of its members studying architecture in Germany. The request

started to turn into reality over coffee at the Technical University of Berlin: Diébédo Francis Kéré from Gando, is a graduate of the Technical University of Berlin. He was asked by his village community to save their school, which was in danger of collapsing.

[1] | Partial front elevation. The idea
is to adapt traditionally temporary
clay building methods to produce
long-term, climatically high quality
results by modifying materials and
construction principles.

[1]

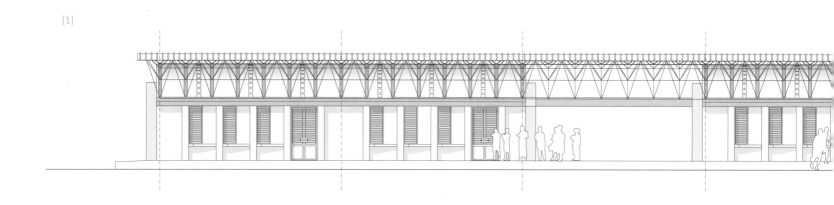

[2] | Side elevation. The building
is covered by a suspended roof
providing protection from sun
and rain.

[3] | Traditional loam construction
methods influence the design of the
building, which also employs new
materials and construction principals.

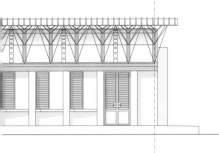

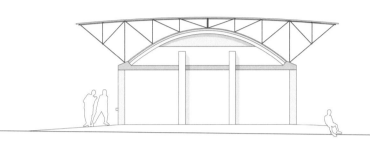

[2]

[3]

[1] | The classrooms are covered by a suspended roof providing protection from sun and rain.
[2] | Building process with the local community.
↘ 250 | Women making a traditional clay floor.

In order to collect money for the new school, Kéré convinced his fellow students to buy one or two symbolic stones for a school in his village in Africa rather than another coffee. He went on to found the 'Schulbausteine für Gando e.V.' association with friends. Its main aim has been the promotion of education, health, and development aid in Gando. The association has been recognised as a charity, a non-profit organisation, since 1999.

The first building was planned for one hundred and twenty pupils. Today, almost three hundred children are waiting to be accepted: thus an extension of the overcrowded school is necessary. The extension of the original project includes not only four classrooms but also a small library. To date, the initiators have not been able to provide every pupil with his or her own set of books. The library building has a rounded shape resembling the traditional clay huts of the region. A kitchen is also planned to complete the ensemble.

The basic principle behind the design was to take the traditional loam building erected as a temporary measure and to turn it into a permanent building of high climatic suitability employing new materials and construction principles. Loam has the great advantage of being an abundant and very cheap material, and of being an integral part of natural life cycles. At the same time, the initiators wished to produce an architectural design that was both modern and aesthetically appealing.

A self-bearing barrel vault was chosen as a soffit for the roof construction. All roofs and walls are manufactured from the compressed clay bricks produced on-site.

The architectural idea was inspired by the tree and the hangar as meeting places and venues for the transfer of knowledge. The classrooms were planned as modular elements so that they could be built in successive stages. This principle enables the construction of schools of any size throughout the whole region.

The shell of the classroom is made of loam and stands on a raised foundation, like the traditional barns used for storing millet. This is covered by a suspended roof to provide protection from sun and rain. The roof has an outer layer of corrugated iron sheets; this thin skin will be kept separate from the solid vault by means of a light construction of thin steel rebars. Air can thus circulate between the two layers; the interaction between the openings in the vault and the tall lamella windows ensures good natural ventilation in the classrooms. The use of reinforcement bars for the roof truss construction prevents the destruction of the roof by termites and is also very economical. Welding is a popular joining technique throughout the entire region.

A key feature of this project is that it was constructed by the labour of the village community alone. All the loam used was local in provenance and all the stabilised loam bricks were produced directly on the building site. The entire roof truss was also built directly on-site using a small welding tool. The key task of the professional workers employed on the construction project was to instruct the young people in the construction techniques used so that the village would be able to undertake its own building projects in the future without the need of outside help.

A further important aspect is the research character of the projects. Cooperation with students from economically and technologically developed Northern Countries allows research to be carried out on-site and for this to be connected with social engagement in a practical way.

121Ethiopia

Hekla Foundation

Private Initiative
Adis Ababa, Ethiopia
2005 (ongoing)

Berlin, Germany
Copenhagen, Denmark

This project is run by the Hekla foundation, which was founded by the artist Olafur Eliasson and the art historian Marianne Krogh Jensen in 2005 with the purpose of improving the lives of many of Ethiopia's orphans.

121Ethiopia is a small organisation with no administrative staff, except for the voluntary board. It consists of a group of professionals from various fields, purposely working on a modest scale, thus allowing them to personally take part at each stage of the aid projects and ensuring that donations are spent as effectively as possible. The foundation puts a great deal of effort into securing the quality of every single project and aims for maximum impact on the lives of those it helps. The purpose of this simple structure is to ensure that all the money donated to the foundation goes solely to its projects in Ethiopia.

Furthermore, the organisation makes demands on the communities it helps: in exchange for its support, it enlists the commitment and active participation of local government and other authorities. This is done, not only to facilitate the integration of the NGO structure, but also in order to give the people in and around the projects a sense of responsibility for their 'involvement' so as to generate local pride and self-esteem.

The renovation and improvement of Kechene Youth Care and Rehabilitation Centre, an orphanage in the Ethiopian capital Addis Ababa, is one of 121Ethiopia current projects. The orphanage was founded in 1955 and is run by the local district government in Addis Ababa. Kechene is home to approximately two hundred young people, from birth to age twenty-two. The building has been undergoing renovation since the end of 2005: 121Ethiopia has installed running water, electricity, new beds and a personal wardrobe for each child. The main building, which houses one hundred twenty girls aged between fourteen and twenty-two, was finished in May 2006. The renovation of the building, which houses the babies and young children (birth to age ten), was completed in September 2006. Furthermore, a cook has been employed to improve the daily life of the children. In October 2006, the renovation of the building that houses children ages ten to fourteen has started. Following the overall renovation of the Kechene orphanage, a comprehensive upgrading of the care and education of all the children will be initiated. This will include staff-training programmes, the employment of more skilled house mothers, the establishment of an efficient infrastructure, the introduction of personal files for each child, sports clubs, notice boards, and a newly built school that all the Kechene children will be able to attend for free, together with children from the neighbourhood.

121Ethiopia is constantly looking for new information and knowledge on how to best help the people in Ethiopia. This approach has helped the small NGO to become very effective. 121Ethiopia delivers the kind of aid that not only makes the greatest impact on the lives of those it helps, but also builds up the children's own sense of involvement and responsibility within the community.

Open Architecture Network

Open Source Internet Platform
2006 (ongoing)

Architecture for Humanity

San Francisco, USA

One billion people live in abject poverty. Four billion live in fragile but growing economies. One in seven people live in slum settlements. By 2020 it will be one in three. The UN Millennium Development Goals aim to 'achieve improvement in the lives of one hundred million slum dwellers by the year 2015'. Reaching this goal will require a profoundly new approach to improving the built environment.

The Open Architecture Network aims to be just such a catalyst for change. The Open Architecture Network is an online, open source community dedicated to improving living conditions through innovative and sustainable design. Here, designers of all persuasions can share their ideas, designs and plans; view and review designs posted by others; collaborate with each other, people in other professions and community leaders in order to address specific design challenges. Furthermore, they can manage design projects from concept to implementation; communicate easily among team members; protect their intellectual property rights using the Creative Commons 'some rights reserved' licensing system, and so be shielded from unwarranted liability and build a more sustainable future.

The Open Architecture Network is the brainchild of Architecture for Humanity and the designers who volunteer with them and through their local Chapters. The network grew out of the collective frustration in sharing ideas and trying to work together to address shelter needs after disaster, in informal settlements and in their own communities. Architecture for Humanity is a charitable organisation that seeks architectural solutions to humanitarian crises and brings design services to communities in need.

The Open Architecture Network is the result of a yearlong partnership that began in spring 2006, when Architecture for Humanity won the prestigious TED (Technology, Entertainment, Design) Prize. Each year the TED community honours three individuals who have a positive impact on life on this planet. The recipients are granted one wish to change the world and members of the TED community voluntarily contribute to granting the wish, by offering their resources and talent. Their wish: to build on their success, creating opportunities for architects to help communities during crises. They envisioned a truly collaborative online community and gathering place for those dedicated to improving the built environment.

Sun Microsystems, Hot Studio, Creative Commons, AMD and other partners joined Architecture for Humanity in realising this ambitious undertaking. Together, at the 2006 TED conference, they launched a beta version of the Open Architecture Network: the first site to offer open source architectural plans and blueprints on the web.

Architects, designers, engineers and anyone else involved in the construction industry is welcome to share their ideas on the network – but the network is not just for professionals – community leaders, non-profit groups, volunteer organisations, government agencies, technology partners, healthcare workers, educators and others are also invited to collaborate on projects and share their expertise.

Far from replacing the traditional architect, the goal of the network is to allow designers to work together in a whole new way, a way that enables five billion potential clients to access their skills and expertise. The network has a simple mission: to generate not one idea but the hundreds of thousands of design ideas needed to improve living conditions for all.

Manuel Martínez Calderón Primary School

School Building
Kathmandu, Nepal
2005 (ongoing)

EMBT Enric Miralles, Benedetta Tagliabue

Barcelona, Spain

[1]

[1] | Model of the interlaced school building
[2] | Collage with conceptual models

The Manuel Martínez Calderón Primary School project is an initiative of The Vicky Sherpa Foundation. The founder of this institution is Victoria Subirana, a Catalan teacher, who, in 1990, decided to carry out a development plan focused on creating quality education for children from the most deprived classes of Nepal. Her vision resulted in the creation of the Eduqual Foundation and the establishment of several projects based on pedagogy, as a tool for the transformation of society. The pedagogical quality of these schools is the stimulus with which positive changes in the lives of the marginalised are promoted.

The foundation is a non-profit, apolitical, non-denominational and non-governmental organisation, whose purpose is the execution of quality educational projects for boys and girls at risk in the most marginalised social classes of Nepal and other areas in the developing world with similar characteristics.

The school is for the so-called 'untouchables' in Nepalese society and the objective is to provide the children with the best educational environment possible.

[2]

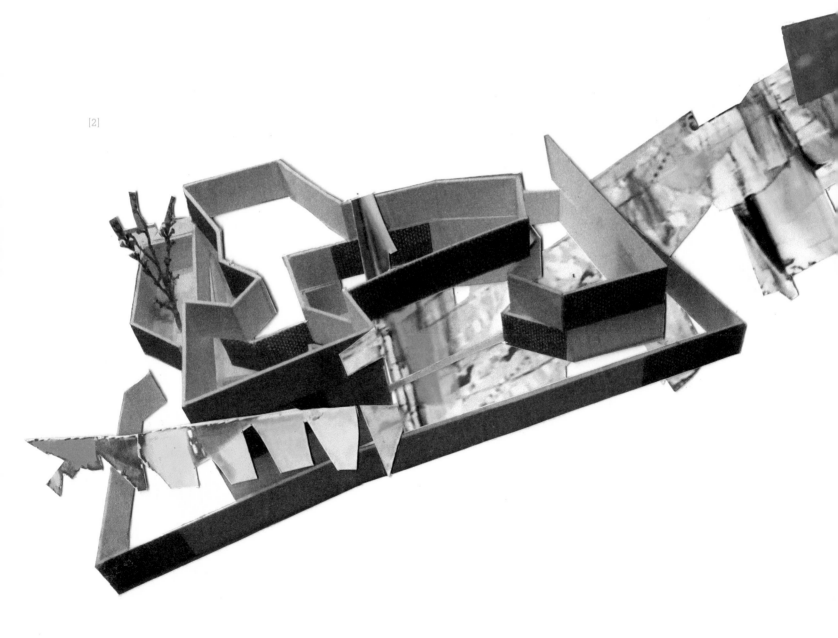

256

| Collage with floor plan and images of the surrounding area displaying the intent to incorporate diverse materials into the façade.

The starting point for the project was a minimal budget and a plot of land that was barely large enough for the proposed building. A river crossing in front of the plot and large abandoned spaces containing accumulations of waste had made the area a marginal zone. This plot of land had great educational potential for the school and the area around it. The implementation of the building in this sector would help to achieve regeneration, not only in the sense of the utilisation of space, but also in the sense of an important civic educational exercise focused on the cleaning of the plot itself and further utilisation as agricultural land, as well as alternative cultivation, job creation, gardening, repair shops and outdoor sports.

Available energy can also be used, as well as electricity that can be generated from the underground fermentation of gases, which are converted into methane gas without the production of smells or environmental degradation. This will be part of a public park that will be thus transformed into a sustainable space.

Earthquake-proof foundations (with a continuous base that covers the whole extent of the plot) were developed to ensure the maximum level of safety. The school project is based on recuperation, recycled and reused materials and the use of waste. The structure permits the incorporation of found or donated materials.

Cross-sections of the four buildings
on the site

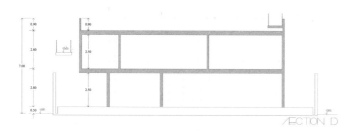

SECTION D

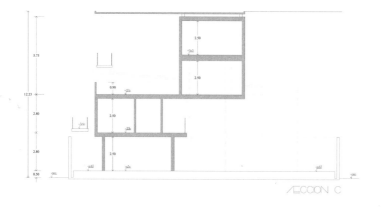

SECCON C

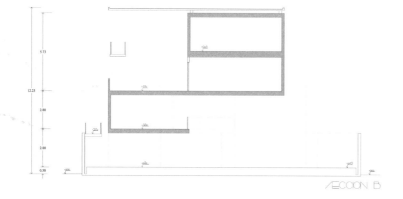

SECCON B

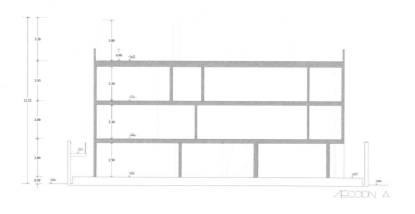

SECCON A

The façades are proposed as an open structure, a kind of anarchic non-composed strip that allows the implementation of recycled materials (bamboo, fabric, coloured bricks) as well as recuperated materials, like various wooden elements and parts used for openings such as doorways and windows. For this purpose. a series of construction details was developed to incorporate various materials into the basic structure. This process is organised in a way that optimises the bioclimatic behaviour of the building.

The advantage of passive energy is optimised in terms of the building orientation, with solid materials forming a natural heat-collecting wall, which regulates the interiour temperature. Cross-ventilation guarantees the building's thermal regulation in a natural way. Solid walls regulate the interiour temperature by taking advantage of differences in day and night temperatures. The incorporation of weight (earth, sand, stones) forms the 'sandwich' system in the interiour of the wall. The two roof types enhance the bioclimatic character: on one side, the green roof improves thermal inertia and, on the other side, the ventilated cavity roof supports for the thermal solar collectors. Rainwater is recuperated to be used for toilets and watering plants.

259 | Concept models. The façades are
        proposed as an open structure, that
        allows the implementation of various
        recycled and recuperated materials.

United Bottle

Recyclable Emergency Shelter
Frankfurt, Germany
2007 (ongoing)

INSTANT
Architects

Zürich, Switzerland
Berlin, Germany

United Bottle is a PET water bottle and a prefabricated building unit. Leading mineral water producers and NGOs use it for water sales or for distribution.

The bottle is integrated into regular PET recycling circuits. It arrives in foiled six-packs on palettes at local shops and is collected and recycled via a bottle deposit system. In emergency situations, the bottles are removed from these circuits and distributed via the UN Refugee Agency (UNHCR) to the respective zones. They are used in combination with a mechanical water pump for local water distribution. 'United Bottle' enables solar drinking-water disinfection (SODIS).

For local distribution, nine bottles form a stabile unit that can be carried by a single person. The tuck-in system generates secure connections that resist torsion. The system is also extremely suitable for use as a building material. In combination with UN tent blankets,

for example, United Bottle acts as a solid shelter construction and as a water reservoir. Filled with local materials such as sand, earth, liquid, and natural insulation materials such as animal hair or feathers, 'United Bottle' becomes a building material for temporary or even long-term shelters.

↘ | Installation of prototype house for the "The Design Annual" 2007 in Frankfurt am Main, Germany.

| The United Bottle scenario is based on the idea that newly designed PET bottles can be taken out of the regular recyling circuits in case of crisis or specific demand, in oder to be used as instant building materials for temporary housing.

Fifty billion PET bottles are currently circulating in Europe alone. Since an obligatory bottle deposit was introduced in Germany in 2003, the return quota has exceeded 90 per cent. PET bottles can be used as returnable bottles or can be recycled, and transformed into a variety of products: from all forms of PET vessels to textiles such as linings and fleece fabrics.

This process – known as 'upcycling' – takes place, for the most part, in China; the final products are resold on the European market. This intersection of local and global circuits forms the basis of this project. Taking the increasing

scarcity of resources into consideration, 'United Bottle' tries to create further recycling circuits in addition to those in existence.

Relief organisations and NGOs face two major challenges during emergencies: the distribution of drinking water and the construction of emergency shelters. In emergencies, the Human Rights Commission or NATO transport tons of technical equipment by air. 'United Bottle' proposes to link consumer goods cycles with those of crisis management to reduce both travel distance and weight. Ideally, 'United Bottle' would already be integrated in local water sales

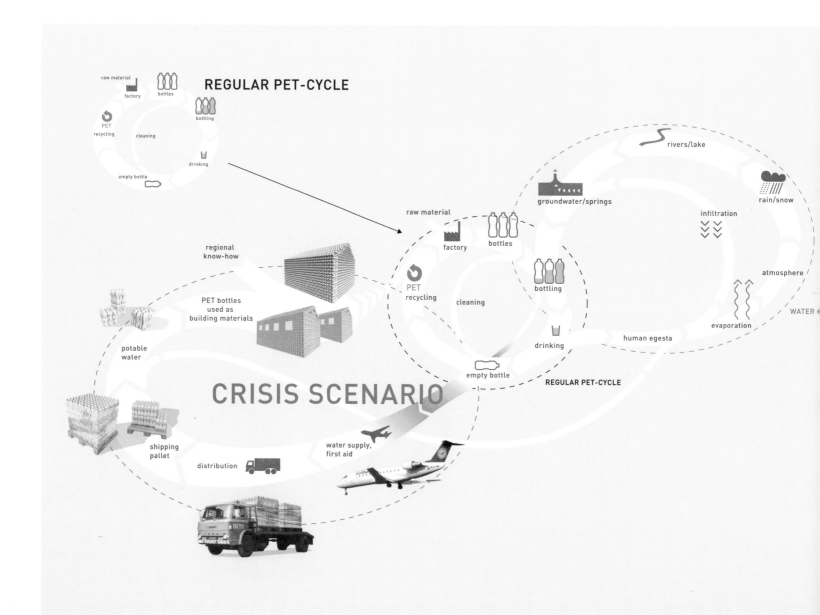

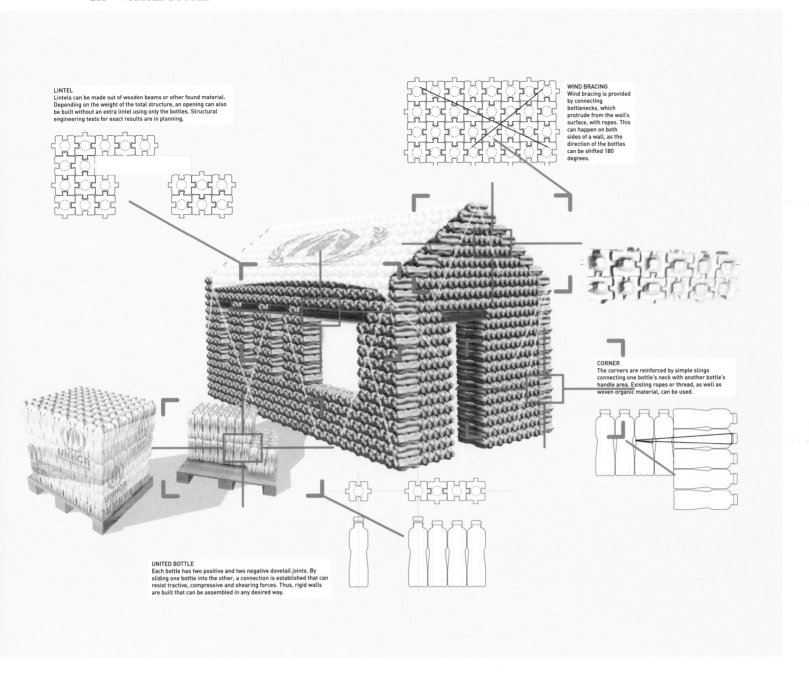

LINTEL
Lintels can be made out of wooden beams or other found material. Depending on the weight of the total structure, an opening can also be built without an extra lintel using only the bottles. Structural engineering tests for exact results are in planning.

WIND BRACING
Wind bracing is provided by connecting bottlenecks, which protrude from the wall's surface, with ropes. This can happen on both sides of a wall, as the direction of the bottles can be shifted 180 degrees.

CORNER
The corners are reinforced by simple slings connecting one bottle's neck with another bottle's handle area. Existing ropes or thread, as well as woven organic material, can be used.

UNITED BOTTLE
Each bottle has two positive and two negative dovetail joints. By sliding one bottle into the other, a connection is established that can resist tractive, compressive and shearing forces. Thus, rigid walls are built that can be assembled in any desired way.

| Construction diagramme

and therefore be immediately available to the local population. A further, crucial advantage of the project, is the opportunities it provides of making use of the local population's technical knowledge to build shelters by reusing prefabricated consumer goods.

The project is currently developing from a thought-provoking conceptual model to a project aiming for implementation. Together with their project partners ETH Zurich (research), Logo Plastic Basel (engineering and optimisation of production processes) and PET-Sachsen (production). Future objectives are the production of a first series of interlocking bottles that will be checked in construction tests for its insulation qualities, structural qualities and long-term material qualities.

Tsunami Safe(r) House

SENSEable City Laboratory

Single House
Sri Lanka
2005 (ongoing)

Massachusetts Institute of Technology
Cambridge, USA

In the wake of the Indian Ocean tsunami disaster of December 2004, most governments in the affected countries announced policies to resettle the population away from the coastline. Building restrictions were proposed to limit reconstruction along the coastal area. Such policies, however, come at high social, cultural, environmental and economic cost. The blanket setback requirements not only suggest arbitrary limitation on reconstruction without acknowledging the geographical/environmental conditions of the sites but also pose structural damage to the local economy of the coastal areas, which depend heavily on fishing and tourism.

The starting point of the Tsunami Safe(r)House project was to find an alternative strategy to resettlement during post-tsunami reconstruction in Sri Lanka. The design team aims to deliver a design that can minimise losses during a tsunami and reduce the difficulty and recovery time of post-disaster reconstruction by substantially improving the structural strength of a residential unit without deviating too much from the typical in terms of form, material, construction method and cost. Through rethinking spatial and structural logic, the design team is able to deliver a 'high-concept, low-technology' design that is five times more able to withstand incoming inundation. Together with an early warning system, the project provides an alternative to resettlement of the population.

Through analysing the collapse mechanism and understanding the structural limitations of the conventional houses, the exteriour enclosure of the building has been redesigned by the 'folding' of the exteriour walls into four structural 'cores' at the corners of the house. The folded walls can resist external impact more effectively as the surface area of the structure directly facing the incoming wave decreases. The cores are folded differently to address different programmatic needs. Furthermore, the infill elements between the cores introduce porosity and allow water to flow around the cores to minimise impacts on the structure.

ROOF COVER
IS MADE OF TIN OR TILES PROVIDES
ECONOMIC PROTECTION AGAINST
RAIN AND SUN

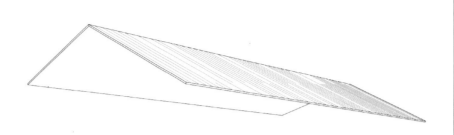

ROOF STRUCTURE
IS MADE OF SIMPLE ELEMENTS
FOLLOWING VERNACULAR
CONSTRUCTION TECHNIQUES

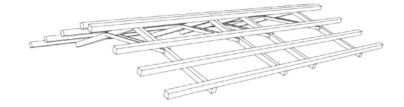

BAMBOO PARTITIONS
CREATE A POROUS AND VENTILATED
SKI, THAT CAN BE UPGRADED BY
RESIDENTS WITH TIME

CORE ELEMENTS
MADE OF CONCRETE BLOCKS
PROVIDE HIGHER RESISTANCE
WITHOUT BLOCKING WATER FLOW IN
CASE OF AN INCOMING TSUNAMI

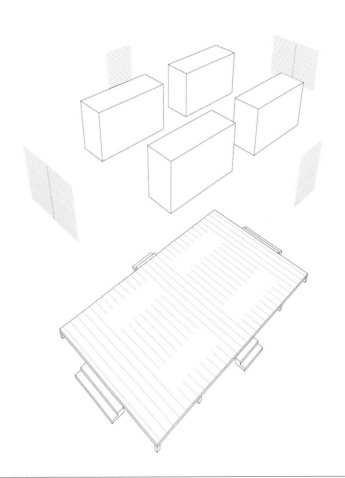

RAISED PLATFORM
IT FACILITATES WATER DRAINAGE
UNDERNEATH AND IT PROVIDES A
HEALTHIER GROUND

↘ | Construction elements of the
Tsunami Safe(r) House. The new
design is not as rigid as traditional
houses, giving more room for water
to flow.

Since the roof stays while the wall resists pressure, the design preserves the basic structure of the house during a tsunami and limits potential damage to the infill elements between the structural cores. As the perimeter opens up, the infill elements introduce lightness against the solidity of the structural cores. From a climatic point of view, the lightness and openness of the perforated infill elements take full advantage of the sea breeze and the tropical sun. Light can penetrate into the heart of the house, and cross-ventilation is optimised by the louvered panels.

The design of the house calls for the use of recycled/local materials. The foundation is built with recycled rubble and cement salvaged from the debris of the adjacent collapsed structure. The walls are constructed with typical concrete blocks (with holes for reinforcement penetration).

The roof takes the form of a traditional pitched roof of 30-degree slope, for better drainage of monsoon rain. The roof tiles are made from local clay, which performs better as a thermal insulator than the alternative corrugated tin roof. The primary roof frame members are all made of solid timber: four horizontal beams span across the width of the house, each of which has a vertical post in the middle to support the ridge beam on top. Roof rafters and purlins are the ubiquitous local coconut fibre members, and they serve as secondary members to support the roof tiles.

In Sri Lanka, families of different generations often live together, rather than creating their own small nuclear family as in most Western cultures. The design of the house provides potential expandability by building additional core elements as families grow. A simple expansion could be linear, with additional cores added to the ends. However, expansion could also happen laterally to form courtyards, resulting in a more complex residential space to better suit individual family members.

The project shows that it is possible to achieve a more structurally, environmentally and economically sustainable design using local construction methods and materials. By re-examining the fundamentals of the conventional Sri Lankan house, this 'high-design, low-technology' strategy provides a new residential prototype that is strongly responsive to the local culture, climate and tradition. It is important to consider that not only a construction problem is being addressed, but also a political and social one: politi-cally, convincing the government of a viable alternative to resettlement and, socially, making people feel safer if they are to remain on the coast. This is exactly the goal of the Tsunami Safe(r) Project.

As a result of The Tsunami Safe(r) Project, 550 from 1,000 planned permanent single-family houses of around 40 square metres each have been constructed in Sri Lanka as part of the post-tsunami reconstruction effort by the Prajnopaya Foundation.

↘ | SENSEable City Laboratory's model for a Sri Lankan house would allow waves to wash through it rather than knocking it flat. The design is up to five times stronger than conventional construction.

Alluvial Sponge Comb

Flood Protection
New Orleans, USA
2006 (ongoing)

Anderson Anderson Architecture

San Francisco, USA

The Alluvial Sponge Comb is a porous, storm-activated seawall and artificial wetland proposal for waterfront cities. Individual fingers of superabsorbent filled fabric structures are deployed along the water's edge as an alternative to the typical concrete flood walls, which often block all passage and view between the city and the river, causing sediment to flush past into the sea without replenishing the urban land mass and so interrupting ecosystems.

During non-storm conditions, the fingers remain separated to allow free passage of people and animals from river to city. During storm conditions the rising water causes the fabric structures to swell and close together into a massive floodwall, slowly shrinking back again as the waters recede. This active porosity mediates between the natural ebb and flow of water and the human inhabitation of urban sites such as New Orleans, Venice, and Bangkok, absorbing and beneficially harnessing nature's impact rather than resisting it.

The design addresses a worldwide infrastructure concern, proposing new modes of waterfront development that accommodate and celebrate natural extremes, avoiding human and ecological destruction while simultaneously contributing to the daily quality of life.

In one of its proposed implementations – at the edge of the Mississippi River in New Orleans – the Alluvial Sponge Comb performs several functions, including flood and erosion control, the slowing of water flow along the riverbank in order to capture silt to aid shoreline build-up, and the sustenance of land and water life – human, plant and animal – by affording both habitat and unencumbered passage through this latent barrier system. In times of unusually high water levels, portions of the comb are designed to swell as they absorb the rising water, becoming a temporary levee to protect the land, people and buildings beyond it. When the floodwaters subside, the swelling in the comb also diminishes and returns the structure to its original fingered form, allowing the riverbank to return to a high degree of porosity. The ideas for this structure are based on considerable research and earlier prototyping of related construction systems.

↘ | The Alluvial Sponge Comb prototype in front of the US pavilion at the 10th International Architecture Biennale in Venice, Italy in 2006.

[1]

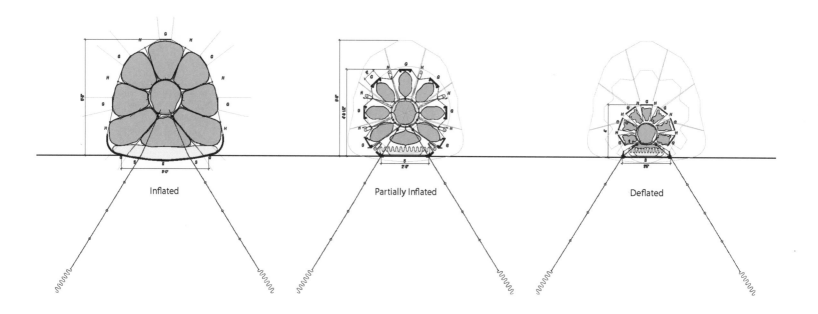

Inflated   Partially Inflated   Deflated

[2]

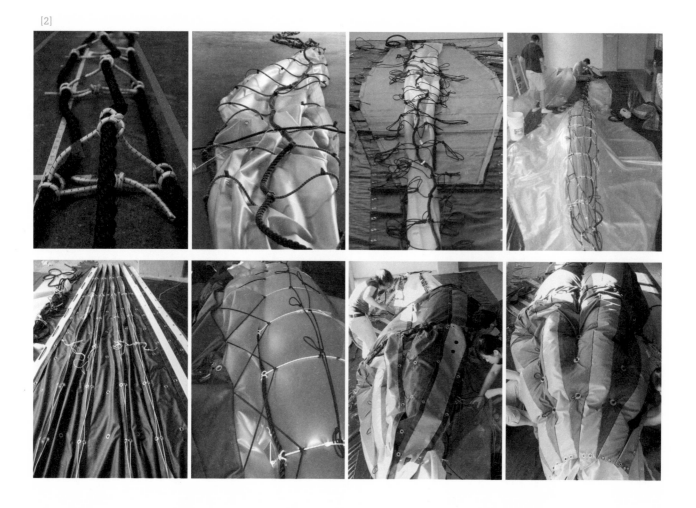

[1] | Cross-sections of a single finger of the Alluvial Sponge Comb
[2] | Building the prototype
[3] | The long 'fingers' of super-absorbant material are deployed along the river's edge. During storm conditions, the rising water causes the 'fingers' to swell together into a massive floodwall.

[3]

In normal weather conditions, the Alluvial Sponge Comb will maintain its slender form, allowing free passage between its open fingers. The major bulk of the fingers will remain on the land, while the long, thin ends of the fingers will dangle in the water, slowing the water enough for eroded earth to settle down and create a soft, welcoming habitat at the water's edge.

During a flood, rising water will reach the superabsorbent fingers through permeable side walls placed under the shingled folds of the top layer of imper-meable fabric. This causes the polymer to absorb up to 1,000 times its weight in water, and to swell into a tightly compressed continuous wall that is anchored by steel cables to steel screw

anchors wound deeply into the earth below, and which sits on a bed of porous geotextile membrane that serves to limit erosion beneath the fingers.

The superabsorbent polymer is reuseable and will be able to swell with water and dry out over many flood cycles. The steel-reinforced elastic interiour harness system and pleated skin is designed to pull back into shape as the polymer dries, without the need for substantial repacking labour.

The cost of fabricating and deploying the Alluvial Sponge Comb should be substantially less than the engineering and construction costs necessary for more conventional flood control systems. The ability to prefabricate off-site, the

easy and rapid transport, and the rapid deployment of the Sponge Comb system makes it ideal for emergency deployment and for international assistance actions in otherwise difficult site conditions. Additionally, the flexibility and eco-friendly porosity of the system make it a supportive and enjoyable component of daily life and urban architecture, 'blossoming' into an effective floodwall only as needed.

project

Solar Updraft
Tower

Solar Thermal Power Plant
La Mancha, Spain
2007 (ongoing)

architects

Schlaich
Bergermann Solar

Stuttgart, Germany

Solar Updraft
Tower

Schlaich
Bergermann Solar

Solar energy can be used in various indirect – biomass, hydropower, wind – and direct forms – e.g. solar thermal power, photovoltaic systems. Sensible technology for the extensive use of renewable energy must be simple and reliable, accessible to the technologically developing countries that receive a lot of sunlight and often have limited raw material resources.

The solar updraft tower meets these conditions. Economic appraisals based on experience and knowledge gathered so far, has shown that large-scale solar updraft towers (≥ 100 MW) are capable of generating electricity at costs comparable to those of conventional power plants.

The solar updraft tower's principle is as follows: air is heated by solar radiation under a low circular transparent or translucent roof open at the periphery; the roof and the ground below form a solar air collector. In the middle of the roof is a vertical tower with large air inlets at its base. The joint between the roof and the tower base is airtight. As hot air is lighter than cold air, it rises up through the tower. Suction from the tower then draws in more hot air from the collector, and cold air comes in from the outer perimeter. Thus, solar radiation causes a constant updraft in the tower. The energy contained in the updraft is converted into mechanical energy by pressure-staged turbines at the base of the tower, and into electrical energy by conventional generators.

[1]

[2]

[1] | A prototype plant with a 200m
tower and 44,000 square metre
collector built in Manzanares, Spain,
in the early eighties was operated
successfully for several years.

[2] | Solar Air Collector of Manzanares
solar updraft tower prototype. The
collector is like a green house. Solar
radiation penetrates the glass, sheet-
plastic or membrane roof and heats the
air under the collector. The lighter hot
air rises through the tower.

Unlike conventional power stations, solar updraft towers do not need cooling water. This is a key advantage in the many sunny countries that already have major water supply problems. The collector uses all solar radiation: both direct and diffuse. This is crucial for tropical countries where the sky is frequently overcast. Due to the soil under the collector working as a natural heat-storage system, solar updraft towers can operate twenty-four hours a day on pure solar energy, with reduced output at night. If desired, additional water tubes or bags, placed under the collector roof, absorb part of the radiated energy during the day and release it into the collector at night. Thus, solar updraft towers can operate as base load power plants.

Solar updraft towers are particularly reliable and not as likely as other power plants to break down. Turbines and generators – subject to a steady flow of air – are the plant's only moving parts. This simple and robust structure guarantees operation that needs little maintenance and, of particular import, no combustible fuel. The building materials needed for solar updraft towers, mainly concrete and glass, are available everywhere in sufficient quantities. In fact, with the energy taken from the solar updraft tower and given the stone and sand available in the desert, these materials can be reproduced on-site. Energy payback time is two to three years. Solar updraft towers can already be constructed even in less industrially developed countries. Existing industries in most countries meet the requirements of solar updraft towers; no investment in high-tech manufacturing plants is needed.

A solar updraft tower generates electricity using direct and diffuse solar radiation. As thermodynamic efficiency increases with tower height, solar updraft towers must be large to generate electricity at competitive cost. Large power plants mean high investment costs. This is due, to a large extent, to the many construction workers required. This in turn means the creation of many jobs, adding value in the country itself.

Solar updraft towers reduce the environmentally disastrous utilisation of dwindling fossil fuels, while removing the need for costly imports of coal, oil and gas, which is especially beneficial for developing countries releasing funds for development.

The construction of solar updraft towers is not associated with resource consumption; resources are merely fixed for a certain time. As solar updraft towers consist mainly of concrete and glass – i.e. sand plus (self-generated) energy – they can reproduce themselves in the desert and are thus a truly sustainable source of energy.

↘ | Concept of a solar updraft tower. Air is heated under a large transparent collector roof. Due to the different densities of warm air inside the collector and ambient cold air, the air inside flows to the centre of the collector roof, and ascends through an updraft chimney in the middle, driving pressure-staged turbines that generate electricity.

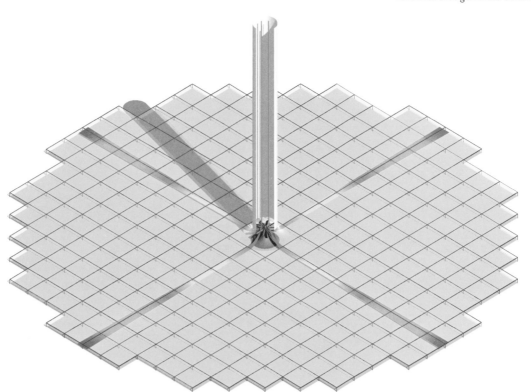

Hawaii Gateway
Energy Centre

Visitors Complex
Kailua-Kona, Hawaii
2005

Ferraro Choi and
Associates

Honolulu, USA

View from the north-east, highlighting spaceframes and thermal chimneys.

[1] | Cross-section.
       1 North space frame, 2 Photovoltaic
       array, 3 Hot air exhaust outlet into
       chimney, 4 Insulated ceiling plenum,
       5 Access flooring, 6 Cool fresh air
       enters, 7 Exhaust inlet,
       8 Cool air outlet, 9 Hawaiian heiau
[2] | Sea water pump design
[3] | Entrance view showing the
       photovoltaic arrays on the space frame.

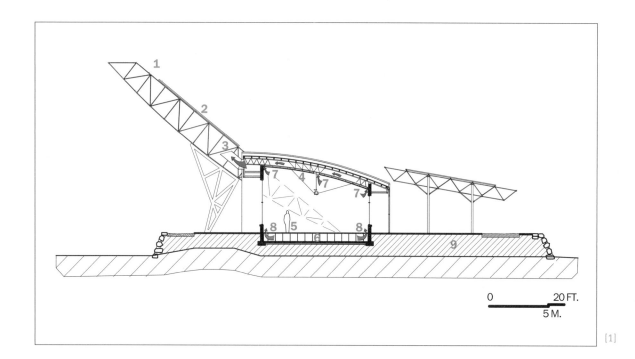

[1]

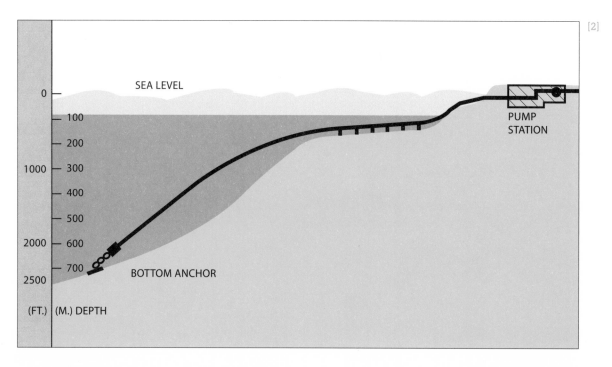

[2]

[3]

The Hawaii Gateway Energy Centre (HGEC) visitor complex, situated on the south coast of Kona on Hawaii's Big Island, serves as the 'gateway' to the Natural Energy Laboratory of Hawaii (NELH), and is the first building to be constructed in what will develop into a 6.5-acre campus of research, development, and demonstration facilities for energy and related high technology fields.

The 330-square metre sustainable visitor complex houses administrative office space, toilets, support areas, and a 185-square metre multi-purpose space that will be utilised for displays, outreach, conferencing, and education. In addition to the visitor complex, Phase 1 includes an initial 185-square metre research

laboratory facility. Phase 2 of the HGEC will add 1,800 square metres of research laboratory space and complete the campus.

The most important sustainable strategy for the HGEC, was to reduce the need for man-made energy sources by utilising building form to harness natural energy systems. In the same sense that a sailing boat is designed to capture wind energy to propel a sleek form through a liquid medium, the HGEC is designed to capture heat and create air movement using only building form and the simple principles of thermodynamics. Thus, the visitor centre is designed as a thermal chimney, moving 100 per cent outside air ventilation at ten to fifteen air changes per hour without the use of a

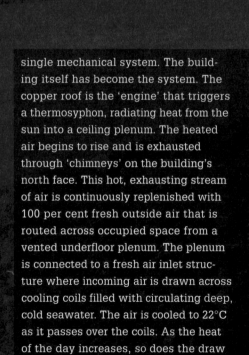

single mechanical system. The building itself has become the system. The copper roof is the 'engine' that triggers a thermosyphon, radiating heat from the sun into a ceiling plenum. The heated air begins to rise and is exhausted through 'chimneys' on the building's north face. This hot, exhausting stream of air is continuously replenished with 100 per cent fresh outside air that is routed across occupied space from a vented underfloor plenum. The plenum is connected to a fresh air inlet structure where incoming air is drawn across cooling coils filled with circulating deep, cold seawater. The air is cooled to 22°C as it passes over the coils. As the heat of the day increases, so does the draw of the thermosyphon, maintaining a

Condensation is collected below the cooling coils and is used for toilet flushing and irrigation of deep-rooted plants. Along with full daylighting during business hours and the elimination of the need for conventional air conditioning, the only energy needs are for the deep seawater circulating pump and the operations plug loads. More than half of this energy is provided by an on-site photovoltaic array that generates 20kWh.

South elevation. Evening view.

Biographies

Anderson Anderson Architecture

Mark Anderson and Peter Anderson started working as a design and build construction company in 1984. Their work focuses on emerging construction technology and prefabrication, as well as on exhibition spaces, new media, and diverse collaborations with artists, scientists and engineers. Mark Anderson teaches at the University of California, Berkeley; Peter Anderson teaches at California College of the Arts. Their firm is based in San Francisco.
www.andersonanderson.com

Architecture for Humanity

Architecture for Humanity, co-founded by architect Cameron Sinclair and Kate Stohr in 1999, is a charitable organisation that seeks architectural solutions to humanitarian crises and brings design services to communities in need. By tapping into a network of professionals willing to lend their time and their talents to helping those who would not otherwise be able to afford their services, Architecture for Humanity supports community development, helps communities rebuild after disaster and provides free design services to community partners around the world.
www.architectureforhumanity.org

BASEhabitat

In 2005, the project studio BASEhabitat – building in developing countries – was set up at the Department of Architecture and Design in the University of Art, Linz in Austria. BASEhabitat stands for basics and beauty, architecture and aesthetics, social and sustainable, energy and education.
www.baseahabitat.ufg.ac.at

Bae Bien-U

Bae Bien-U is an internationally renowned photographer from South Korea. Since the early 1980s, he has concentrated on the pine forests found across all of South Korea.
www.galerie-poller.com

Borries, Friedrich von

Friedrich von Borries, born 1974 in Berlin, Germany, studied architecture in Berlin, Brussels and Karlsruhe, where he received his PhD in 2004. He has taught architectural and urban design at the Bauhaus Dessau Foundation, the Technical University Berlin and the ETH Zurich, Switzerland. Since 2007 he has been Visiting Professor for Art and Public Space at the Academy of Arts, Nuremberg. Together with Matthias Böttger, he runs the Berlin-based architectural office raumtaktik, which works in the fields of spatial reconnaissance and intervention.
www.raumtaktik.de

Carlo Ratti Associati

Carlo Ratti Associati – Walter Nicolino and Carlo Ratti – is a rapidly growing architectural office that begain in 2002 in Turin, Italy. It draws on Carlo's research at the Massachusetts Institute of Technology and is currently involved in a number of architecture schemes, both nationally and internationally.
www.carloratti.com

Chang, Yung Ho

Yung Ho Chang, born in 1956 in Beijing, China. He is Professor of Architecture and Head of the Department of Architecture at the Massachusetts Institute of Technology (MIT) in Boston. He came from Peking University where he was Head and Professor of the Graduate Centre of Architecture. He received his MA from the University of California at Berkeley and taught in the US for fifteen years before returning to Beijing to establish China's first private architecture firm, Atelier FCJZ.
www.fcjz.com, www.architecture.mit.edu

DesignInc

The Australian architecture office DesignInc focuses on creating quality environments that reconcile natural, social, and economic imperatives. DesignInc is committed to ecologically sustainable design, by applying passive design strategies, renewable energy, and material selection in ways that support the continuity of the natural environment.
www.designinc.com.au

Dougherty, Patrick

Combining his carpentry skills with his love for nature, he began to learn more about 'primitive' techniques of building and experimented with tree saplings as a construction material. Over the last decade he has built over one hundred works throughout the United States, Europe and Asia.
www.stickwork.net

Ecosistema Urbano

[ecosistema urbano] is an architecture and engineering team that focuses on the research and ecological design of new architecture projects that understand sustainable development as a resource for innovation and enthusiasm.
www.ecosistemaurbano.com

EMBT, Miralles Tagliabue

In 1991, Benedetta Tagliabue and Enric Miralles started working together and soon became partners. In 1998 they founded Miralles Tagliabue EMBT in Barcelona. Their work includes representative buildings and public spaces in Barcelona as well as in other European cities. EMBT is currently working for state and local governments, as well as corporate and private clients. EMBT's architecture has been awarded multiple international awards.
www.mirallestagliabue.com

Engineers Without Borders (EWB)

Engineers Without Borders (EWB) is a non-profit humanitarian organisation established to partner with developing communities worldwide in order to improve their quality of life. This partnership involves the implementation of sustainable engineering projects, while involving and training internationally responsible engineers and engineering students. The Yale Chapter of EWB is an undergraduate organisation made up of students from a variety of backgrounds. We also have extremely dedicated professional mentors and faculty advisors. We draw strength from diversity, imagination and commitment.
www.ewb-international.org

Fabrizio, Leo

The photographer Leo Fabrizio displays an unusual talent for uniting natural and urban landscapes in space and time. His current work-in-progress *Dreamworld*, focuses on Southwest Asia and on the irrational exuberance of the building/demolition that inevitably dominates a natural landscape abandoned to its own fate.
www.leofabrizio.com

Feireiss, Kristin

Kristin Feireiss, born 1942 in Berlin, Germany, founded the Aedes Architecture Forum in Berlin in 1980, now one of the most successful institutions internationally for communicating architectural culture, urban design and similar topics. She acted as the Director of the Netherlands Architecture Institute from 1996 to 2001 and has edited numerous publications in the field of architecture.
www.aedes-arc.de

Feireiss, Lukas

Lukas Feireiss, born 1977 in Berlin, Germany, attained his graduate education in Religious Studies, Philosophy and Ethnology with a specific focus on the relationship between architecture and other fields of knowledge and experience. As a teacher, writer and curator he has been deeply involved in the discussion and mediation of architecture, art and media beyond its disciplinary boundaries.
www.lukasfeireiss.com

Ferraro Choi And Associates

Ferraro Choi And Associates is an architectural firm located in Honolulu, Hawaii. Established in 1988 by Joseph Ferraro, AIA and Gerald Choi, AIA, the firm gained its initial reputation in interiour architecture for its work designing corporate office environments in Honolulu. Since 2000, Ferraro Choi has focused on sustainable design. Since 2003, the firm's principals have been Joseph Ferraro, AIA, William Brooks, AIA and Troy Miyasato, AIA.
www.ferrarochoi.com

Fried, David

Born 1962 in NYC, the artist David Fried reveals complex dynamic relationships in the form of minimalist dichotic images and objects. His exploration into the inherent qualities and flexible characteristics of interdependent-networked systems found in nature and social endeavour are echoed throughout his sculptural, photographic and interactive works.
www.davidfried.com

Fundamentals of Ecological Planning and Building

The department Fundamentals of Ecological Planning and Building was established in 1997. It is conceived not as a conventional subject area, but as an interdisciplinary unit that aims to bring together activities in the field of building and the environment; working across the boundaries of individual disciplines and aiming to identify and develop principles and tendencies. Ecological planning and building extends beyond individual disciplines and should become a fixed, interdisciplinary component of both the teaching curriculum and research.
www.uni-weimar.de/architektur/
oekologisches_bauen

Grüntuch Ernst Architekten

Almut Ernst, born 1966 in Stuttgart, Germany and Armand Grüntuch, born 1963 in Riga, Latvia, founded their Berlin-based practice in 1991. The projects realised by Grüntuch Ernst Architects have been published in numerous publications and awarded national and international prizes. In 2006, they had the honour of being commissioned to create the German contribution to the 10th International Architecture Biennale in Venice.
www.gruentuchernst.de

GrAT - Centre for Appropriate Technology

The main office of GrAT is located at Vienna Technical University in the centre of Vienna and a branch office, the Böheimkirchen Centre for Appropriate Technology (BÖZAT), is located in Lower Austria near the regional capital of St. Pölten. GrAT is a scientific association that consists of an interdisciplinary team of experts: architects, process engineers, biologists, machine engineers, computer experts and agricultural experts. The group is linked by the awareness of joint responsibility for socially and ecologically beneficial interaction with technology and its consequences. Modern technological research needs attractive innovations that focus on a new quality of life and which combine functional and ecological advantages.
www.grat.at

Halso, Ilkka

Ilkka Halso, born 1965 in Orimattila, Finland. He works with themes concerning scientific illustration and methods of natural history research. His work has essentially been a small investigation of the visual world of science. Recently, his interest has focused more on the various relations between architecture/technology and nature.
ilkka.halso.net

Haverstock Associates LLP

Haverstock Associates LLP is a design-led practise, formed in 1980, with a simple vision of creating buildings that inspire and stimulate. The practise consists of four partners who oversee a staff of fifteen architects and architectural assistants, as well as three administrative staff. Sustainability, consultation and process management are key to the approach of the practise to designing buildings.
www.haverstock.com

Heijdens, Simon

London-based Dutch ambient designer Simon Heijdens implements technology in subtle ways and produces high-profile works. He reveals a fascination with the role objects play in our society and the ways in which our perception of them can be changed.
www.simonheijdens.com

Hekla Foundation

121Ethiopia.org is a project of the Hekla foundation, which was founded by Olafur Eliasson and Marianne Krogh Jensen in 2005. It is a small organisation with no administrative staff, except for the voluntary board. The purpose of this simple structure is to ensure that all money donated to the foundation goes solely to its projects in Ethiopia.
www.121Ethiopia.org

Herringer, Anna

Anna Herringer, born 1977 in Rosenheim, Germany, is an architect who developed the METI School in Bangladesh as part of her PhD thesis at the University of Art, Linz. Herringer is currently working on her PhD at the Technical University of Munich. She has just finished the second project phase in Bangladesh: a vocational school and a pilot project on rural housing.
www.meti-school.de

Ingenhoven Architects

Christoph Ingenhoven founded the Ingenhoven Architects architectural studio in 1985. His office has won numerous prizes in international competitions, including many first prizes and many awards for completed projects and their ecological and sustainable approach. Christoph Ingenhoven is one of the world's leading architects in designing sustainable and ecological architecture.
www.ingenhovenarchitekten.de

INSTANT Architects

Dirk Hebel and Jörg Stollmann are the principals of INSTANT Architects in Zurich, founded in 2002. INSTANT foregrounds the body as a biological and social construct in order to develop research projects and architectural practice on a range of scales. Both partners were trained at Princeton University and worked for various architecture offices in New York, Paris and Berlin. They have held teaching positions at UdK Berlin, TU Berlin, the American University of Sharjah, Syracuse University, and Princeton University, as well as ETH Zurich.
www.instant-arch.net

Kéré, Diébédo Francis

Diébédo Francis Kéré is a young architect from Burkina Faso who studied in Berlin, Germany. Assisted by friends, he founded the *Schulbausteine für Gando Association* while still a student. The association's aims are to create buildings that meet climatic demands, and to support Burkina Faso's inhabitants in their development. As well as his work in his own architecture office, he is also lecturer at the Technical University of Berlin.
www.fuergando.com

KieranTimberlake Associates

For over two decades, KieranTimberlake Associates has been recognised for its research-based practice that focuses on new materials, processes, assemblies and products. The firm's approach to improving the art, quality and craft of architecture is illustrated in *Manual: The Architecture of KieranTimberlake*. Their influential book *Refabricating Architecture*, investigates how transfer processes from aerospace, auto and ship manufacturers are poised to transform architecture.
www.kierantimberlake.com

KOL/MAC LLC

KOL/MAC LLC is a professional architecture and design firm based in New York City and also operates internationally. Widely acknowledged as a leader in architecture and design for its innovative digital approach, the firm's current work is focused on linking unique digital design methods to new methods of construction, new technologies of production and a new generation of materials. While always forward-looking and progressive, the firm is equally sensitive to the programmatic, situational and socio-economic conditions that define each project.
www.kolmaclcc.com

Limited Design

The Beijing-based architecture firm Limited Design was founded in 2006 by Chinese architect Wang Hui.

Ludwig, Andreas

Andreas Ludwig is Chairman of the Executive Board and Chief Executive Officer of Zumtobel Group, a leading global lighting company, headquartered in Austria. Before assuming this responsibility at Zumtobel Group, Ludwig was Managing Director of UBS Warburg, one of the world's leading international investment banks, based in London.
www.zumtobelgroup.com

LURI.watersystems.GmbH

Founded in 2006 by Ralf Steeg together with the project developer Klaus Gabrielli, LURI. watersystems develops new water treatment technologies that unite environmental protection, water management, architecture and urban development.
www.luritec.com

Lyons Architects

Lyons is an architectural and urban design practise, based in Melbourne, Australia. The firm is committed to the craft of architecture and urban design as an intellectual construct within a local and global culture. Lyons proposes an architecture that is confident and self-conscious about its cultural origins and which embodies the complexities of invention, ideas and identity. Lyons was established in 1996 and is led by its three directors, Corbett Lyon, Cameron Lyon and Carey Lyon and its four Principals, Neil Appleton, Adrian Stanic, Peter Bartlett and Rob Tursi.
www.lyonsarch.com.au

Mario Cucinella Architects

MCA, Mario Cucinella Architects, founded in 1992 in Paris and in Bologna in 1999, is a company with solid experience at the forefront of contemporary design and research. Mario Cucinella, with his partner Elizabeth Francis, leads an international team of architects, engineers and designers. Sustainable building design and the rational use of energy is one of the central concerns of MCA's work and research.
www.mca-architects.com

McDonough, William

William McDonough, born 1952 in Tokyo, Japan, is an American architect and designer. He is the founding principal of William McDonough + Partners, Architecture and Community Design, an internationally recognised design firm practising ecologically, socially, and economically intelligent architecture and planning in the US and abroad. He is also the co-founder and principal, with German chemist Michael Braungart, of McDonough Braungart Design Chemistry (MBDC), which employs a comprehensive Cradle-to-Cradle design protocol to chemical benchmarking, supply-chain integration, energy and materials assessment, clean-production qualification, as well as sustainability issue management and optimisation.
www.mcdonough.com

Méchain, François

François Méchain was born in Varaize, France in 1948. The photographer and sculptor has been teaching photography and the history of photography at the Saint-Etienne Arts and Design International School since 1977. Since 1996, he has been in charge of a sculpture course at Jean Monnet University, Saint-Etienne. He has exhibited worldwide.
www.francoismechain.com

Morgan, Paul

Paul Morgan is director of the Melbourne-based practice Paul Morgan Architects. PMA's work explores the idea of 'performance shells', mainly in the types of educational, institutional buildings and urban design. PMA's projects have been extensively published nationally and internationally and the Cape Schanck House was recently awarded the 2007 National RAIA Robin Boyd award for residential architecture. Paul has taught at the School of Architecture at RMIT since 1989 and has worked as the editor of renowned RMIT publications *Transition* and *38 South*.
www.paulmorganarchitects.com

Morphosis

Morphosis, a Los Angeles-based practise founded and directed by American architect Thom Mayne, is a dynamic and evolving architectural practise that responds to the shifting and advancing social, cultural, political and technological conditions of modern life. Morphosis is one of the most prominent design practises, with completed projects worldwide. For his architectural work, Thom Mayne was awarded the Pritzker Prize in 2005.
www.morphosis.net

Nash, David

David Nash (1945) is an artist, internationally renowned for working with wood to create large, dramatic and tactile sculptures. He lives in North Wales and has created a significant body of work in which the relationship between man and nature is a central theme .

Nils-Udo

Nils-Udo was born in Lauf, Germany, in 1937. After working as a painter in Paris, he chose to work directly with natural elements in 1972. Since then he has made a great many site-specific installations all over the world using leaves, branches and logs, berries and any other organic materials that he finds in the place where he is working. The beauty of nature is revealed in his work via the manipulation and alteration caused by the intervention of the artist. In the 1980s he began to show his works all over the world in group and solo shows.

Opera Bosco

The Belgian artist Anne Demijttenaere started working with Art in Nature in 1994, at the same time creating the open-air Museum Opera Bosco on two hectares of woods in the natural protection area of Calcata, Italy in the province of Viterbo. All the site-specific works of art there, are realised exclusively using local raw natural materials or raw material 'invited' from other places.
www.operabosco.com

Petersen, Matt

Matt Petersen is the President and CEO of Global Green USA and serves on the board of the company. Petersen joined Global Green USA in 1994 and is the Chair of the Green Cross International Energy and Resource Efficiency programme. Petersen drives and guides Global Green USA's new programmes, including the organisation's green rebuilding initiative in New Orleans, which included a sustainable design competition chaired by Brad Pitt.
www.globalgreen.org

Public Architecture

Founded by American architect John Peterson of Peterson Architects in 2002, Public Architecture puts the resources of architecture in the service of the public interest. They identify and solve practical problems of human interaction in the built environment and act as a catalyst for public discourse through education, advocacy and the design of public spaces and amenities.
www.publicarchitecture.org

Rafael Viñoly Architects

Rafael Viñoly Architects began with the founding of the New York office in 1983, and has since become known internationally for its architectural projects around the globe. In addition to site offices, the firm now has affiliated offices in London and Los Angeles. Rafael Viñoly Architects has designed a number of landmark cultural and civic complexes as well as laboratories and master plans.
www.rvapc.com

Roswag, Eike

Eike Roswag, born 1969 in Gießen, Germany, is an architect working in a Berlin-based internationally active network for sustainable buildings with a focus on natural materials and energy efficiency, and teaches at the Technical University of Berlin. Eike Roswag joined Anna Herringer for the implementation of the METI School project in Bangladesh.
www.werk-a.de

Rural Studio

Auburn School of Architecture's Rural Studio is an off-campus educational and outreach program based in the Black Belt region of West

Alabama, which is known for the colour of its rich agricultural soil. Samuel Mockbee, founder with D.K. Ruth and the first Rural Studio director, envisioned a setting in which students learned by building projects of their own design while simultaneously serving and learning in communities with which they are most often unfamiliar. This is a place for students to discover for themselves what Mockbee meant by 'citizen architect' through their work and by immersion in the cultural richness of this place and its people.
www.ruralstudio.com

Sassen, Saskia

Saskia Sassen, born 1949 at The Hague, Netherlands, is currently the Lynd Professor of Sociology and Member of The Committee on Global Thought at Columbia University. She held various other academic positions both in and outside the USA, such as the Ralph Lewis Professor of Sociology at the University of Chicago and the Centennial Visiting Professor of Political Economy in the Department of Sociology at the London School of Economics. She has just completed a five-year project for Unesco on sustainable human settlement with a network of researchers and activists in over 30 countries.
www.sociology.columbia.edu

Schaik, Leon van

Leon van Schaik is Innovation Professor of Architecture at the Royal Melbourne Institute of Technology (RMIT). From his base in Melbourne, he has promoted local and international architectural culture through practice-based research. In 2006, Leon van Schaik was awarded an Order of Australia,

Officer (AO) in the General Division, for service to architecture as an academic, practitioner and educator, and to the community through involvement with a wide range of boards and organisations related to architecture, culture and the arts.
www.leonvanschaik.com

Schlaich Bergermann Solar

Schlaich Bergermann and Partners, Stuttgart, Germany are independent consultant civil and structural engineers. The consultancy strives to design sophisticated engineering structures ranging from wide-span lightweight roofs, a diversity of bridges and slender towers to innovative solar energy power plants.
www.sbp.de

SENSEable City Laboratory

The SENSEable City Laboratory is a research initiative at the Massachusetts Institute of Technology, directed by Carlo Ratti. The critical study and anticipation of the impact of new tools for, and new developments in architecture, design and urban planning are their core research interests.
www.senseable.mit.edu

Sauerbruch Hutton Architects

Matthias Sauerbruch and Louisa Hutton founded their architectural practice in London in the late eighties. A second office was opened in Berlin in 1993. With large-scale projects completed in Berlin and elsewhere, Sauerbruch Hutton has begun to redefine the notion of ecologically aware construction. The concern for the economical use of resources – both

natural and urban – is juxtaposed and extended into the idiosyncratic treatment of spaces on all scales.
www.sauerbruchhutton.de

SMC Alsop

SMC Alsop is committed to architecture of delight and enjoyment, attained through a process that involves the building users, the client and the local community. Community involvement is seen as a vital ingredient in the design process. In addition, SMC Alsop's buildings are known for their bold and often dramatic incorporation of art that reinforces the innovative use of new materials and the bold use of colour. SMC Alsop has its principal office in London, together with offices in Shanghai Beijing and Singapore.
www.smcalsop.com

Sobek, Werner

Werner Sobek Engineering and Design is an international consultancy that operates on a worldwide scale. The firm has offices in Germany (Stuttgart, Frankfurt), the USA (New York), Russia (Moscow), and the Middle East (Cairo, Dubai, Khartoum). All firms realise numerous projects in the areas of structural engineering, façade engineering, green technologies and design. The full range of the company's services are available in all of its offices. The group was founded by Professor Werner Sobek in 1992.
www.wernersobek.com

Steeg, Ralf

Qualified Engineer Ralf Steeg, born in 1961, is a landscape architect. Since 2001, Ralf Steeg, now sponsored by the German Federal Ministry

of Education and Research, has been working
with his partner Klaus Gabrielli and a team of
twenty-four engineers, historians, economists,
artists, architects and communications experts
on cleaning the River Spree in Berlin.
www.spree2011.de

Steven Holl Architects

Steven Holl was born in 1947 in Bremerton,
Washington and established STEVEN HOLL
ARCHITECTS in New York City in 1976.
Considered one of America's most important architects, Steven Holl is recognised for his ability
to blend space and light with great contextual
sensitivity and to utilise the unique qualities of
each project to create a concept-driven design.
He specialises in seamlessly integrating new
projects into contexts with particular cultural
and historic importance.
www.stevenholl.com

Töpfer, Klaus

Klaus Töpfer, born 1938, is a German politi-
cian and environmental politics expert. In
1998, Töpfer was appointed Under-Secretary
General of the United Nations, General
Director of the United Nations office in
Nairobi and Executive Director of the United
Nations Environment Programme (UNEP). He
held several posts in the Federal Government
of Germany such as the Federal Minister
of Regional Planning, Building and Urban
Development from 1994 to 1998, Federal
Minister of Environment, Nature Conservation
and Nuclear Energy from 1987 to 1994. Before
his political career, Klaus Töpfer was Full
Professor at the University of Hanover where
he directed the Institute of Regional Research
and Development.

Turell, James

James Turell, born 1943, Los Angeles, is an
American artist primarily concerned with
light and space. He is best known for his work
in progress, Roden Crater. Located outside
Flagstaff, Arizona, Turell is turning this natural
cinder volcanic crater into a massive naked-eye
observatory, designed specifically for the viewing of celestial phenomena.

Urban-Think Tank

The Urban-Think Tank is an international
design practice dedicated to the research and
practice in the field of contemporary design
in architecture, urbanism and socio-cultural
issues addressing organisation, identity and
programme in emerging urban centres. U-TT
was founded in Caracas, Venezuela in 1993
by Alfredo Brillembourg and in 1998, Hubert
Klumpner joined as partner. In 2003, U-TT
expanded its activities by adding a New York
teaching and research branch at the Columbia
University architecture school where U-TT
runs the SLUMLAB.COM (Sustainable Living
Urban Model).
www.u-tt.com

World Wildlife Fund UK

As part of the international WWF network,
WWF-UK addresses global threats to people
and nature such as climate change, the peril to
endangered species and habitats, and the un-
sustainable consumption of the world's natural
resources. WWF-UK does this by influencing
the way that governments, businesses and
people think, learn and act in relation to the
world around us, and by working with local
communities to improve their livelihoods and

the environment upon which we all depend.
WWF uses its practical experience, knowledge
and credibility to create long-term solutions for
the planet's environment.
www.wwf.org.uk

Yeang, Ken

Ken Yeang, born in Penang, Malaysia. He is a
prolific Malaysian architect, writer and ecologist best known for developing environmental
design solutions in architecture and urbanism.
He is the principal of the UK-based practice
Llewelyn Davis Yeang and author of the seminal book *Ecodesign. Instruction Manual for
Ecological Design*. His work is distinguished by
its cutting-edge research, design and development, concerned with the bioclimatic design of
high-rise buildings.
www.llewelyn-davies-ltd.com

Youmeheshe

Youmeheshe is an architectural practice
formed to design buildings and environments
of significance that benefit the lives of people
who use them. Youmeheshe was founded in
05.05.05. by Simon Beames and Simon Dickens
who have worked together closely for eighteen
years. Youmeheshe is an ethical practice with
regard to trade, ecology and sustainability.
www.youmeheshe.com

Credits

Rainscape No.41
David Fried
000   2005, Archival C-print, Plexiglas,
UV silicon, Alu-Dibond, Aluminium. 86 x 115 cm.

Brioude
François Méchain
000   1999, Black and white photograph on
PVC, 199 x 95.5 cm. In situ ephemeral sculpture,
oak trees and grasses from the meadow:
10.5 x 7 x 3.50 m. Courtesy Galerie Michèle
Chomette, Paris

Chambre d'écoute
François Méchain
001   2003-2004, Digne les Bains, Haute
Provence, France. Black and white photograph
on aluminium: 115 x 115 cm. In situ, ephemeral
sculpture, birch tree, plane tree leaves, strong
smells: 7 x 4.9 x 2.8. Courtesy Galerie Michèle
Chomette, Paris

Clemson Clay-Nest
Nils-Udo
002   2005, Clemson, Botancial Garden
of South Carolina, Fuji Flex on Aluminium,
111 x 126 cm, edition 8

Root Sculpture
Nils-Udo
003   1995, Chapultepec Park, Mexico City.
Fuji Flex on Aluminium, 124 x 1124 cm, edition 3

Manglas
Nils-Udo
004-005   2005, Maracaibo, Venezuela.
Fuji Flex on Aluminium, 66.5 x 100 cm, edition 8

New and old door
Opera Bosco
006   1995-2006, Opera Bosco Museo di Arte
nella Natura - Calcata, Italy. Vitalba 330 x 100 x 350 cm.
Photographer: Anne Demijttenaere

Holy Rope
Patrick Dougherty
007   1992, Rinjyo-in Temple, Chiba, Japan;
hight 7.62 m. Reeds and bamboo.
Photographer: Tadahisa Sakurai

Na Hale 'o waiawi
Patrick Dougherty
008-009   2003, Contemporary Art Museum,
Honolulu, Hawaii. Photographer: Paul Kodama

Ash Dome
David Nash
010   since 1977, Cae'n-y-Coed, North
Wales, U.K.; Courtesy Galerie Scheffel & Artist
Photographer: Christian Scheffel

Around the Corner
Patrick Dougherty
011   2003, University of Southern Indiana,
New Harmony Gallery, New Harmony, IN, USA.
Photographer: Doyle Dean

Cape Schanck House
Paul Morgan Architects
052-059   Photographer: Peter Bennetts

OKO House
Youmeheshe Architects
60-63

H16
Werner Sobek
64-71   Photographer: Zooey Braun,
Stuttgart /Germany

Lufthansa Aviation Center
Ingenhoven Architekten
72-79   Photographer: H. G. Esch, Hennef

Palestra Building
SMC Alsop
80-85   Photographer: Christian Richters

CH2 Melbourne City Council House
DesignInc
86-91   Credits: The City of Melbourne in
association with DesignInc Melbourne,
Photographer: Dianna Snape

Parliament Hill School
Haverstock Associates LLP
92-97   Photographer: ©Dennis Gilbert/VIEW

Marie Curie High School
Grüntuch Ernst Architekten
98-105   Photographer: Werner Huthmacher

1% Solution
Public Architecture
106

Ecological Budget UK
World Wildlife Fund UK
107

Valley View University
Chair for Fundamentals of Ecological Planning
and Building
108-109

SPREE2011
Ralf Steeg & LURI.watersystems.GmbH
110-113   Credits: LURI©Sven Flechsenhar

Metro Cable San Augustin
Urban-Think Tank
114-119   Credits: Alfredo Brillembourg &
Hubert Klumpner
116   Graphic design: Ruedi Baur

Ecoboulevard
Ecosistema Urbano
120-127   Photographer: Emilio P. Doiztua

S-House
GrAT - Centre for Appropriate Technology
142-145

METI School
Anna Herringer, Eike Roswag
146-153   Photographer: Kurt Hörbst

Ali Apple Elementary School
Limited Design
154-157

Sidwell Friends Middle School
KieranTimberlake Associates
158-160   Photographer: © Barry Halkin
161-163   Photographer: © Peter Aaron / Esto

DPI Queenscliff Centre
Lyons Architects
164-169   Photographer: John Gollings
Photography

Howard Hughes Medical Institute
Rafael Vinoly Architects
170-173   Photographer: © Brad Feinknopf
174 [1]   Photographer: Jeff Goldberg / Esto
174 [2]   Photographer: Paul Warchol
175   Photographer: Jeff Goldberg / Esto
177   Photographer: Paul Fetters

SIEEB
Mario Cucinella Architects
178-179   Photographer: Daniele Domenicali
180 [1]   Photographer: Alessandro Digaetano
181 [2]   Photographer: Daniele Domenicali
181 [3]   Photographer: Alessandro Digaetano
183   Photographer: Daniele Domenicali

Whitney Water Purification Facility and Park
Steven Holl Architects
184-185   Photographer: Paul Warchol
186   Photographer: Chris McVoy
187 [2]   Photographer: Michael van
Valkenburgh Associates
187 [3]   Photographer: Chris McVoy
187 [4]   Photographer: Steven Holl Architects
188-189   Photographer: Paul Warchol

Federal Environmental Agency
Sauerbruch Hutton Architects
190-197 [1] Photographer: Jan Bitter, bitterbredt.de
197 [2]   Photographer: Busse GmbH

San Francisco Federal Building
Morphosis
198-199   Photographer: Roland Halbe
200-201   Photographer: Nic Lehoux
203 [2]   Photographer: Roland Halbe
203 [3]   Photographer: Nic Lehoux
204-206   Photographer: Nic Lehoux
207   Photographer: Roland Halbe
208-209   Photographer: Nic Lehoux

INVERSAbrane
KOL / MAC LCC
210-211   Credits: Architects: KOL / MAC, LLC
Sulan Kolatan and William Mac Donald
Photographer: Installation photographs provided
by DuPont USA

New Monte Rosa-Hut
Studio Monte Rosa / ETH Zürich
212-215   Architects: Studio Monte Rosa,
Prof. Andrea Deplazes, Marcel Baumgartner,
Kai Hellat, Department of Architecture, ETH Zurich
Project partners: ETH Zurich and Swiss Alpine
Club (SAC)

20K $ House
Rural Studio
232-233   Photographer: Timothy Hursley
235 [3]   Photographer: Alexandre Landry
235 [4]   Photographer: Timothy Hursley

Kikoo Water Project
Engineers Without Borders
236-239

Living Tebogo
BASEhabitat
240   Credit: Kunstuniversität Linz

241-243   Photographer: Sabine Gretner
242   Credit: Kunstuniversität Linz
243   Credit: Richard Steger

Schulbausteine für Gando e.V.
Diébédo Francis Kéré
244-251

121Ethiopia
Hekla Foundation
252

Open Architecture Network
Architecture for Humanity
253

Manuel Martínez Calderón Primary School
EMBT - Enric Miralles, Benedetta Tagliabue
254-259

United Bottle
INSTANT Architects
260-263   Photographer: Constantin Meyer,
Cologne

Tsunami Safe(r) House
SENSEable City Laboratory
264-267   Advisor: Tenzin Priyadarshi
Design team: Luis Berrios Negron, Justin Lee,
Walter Nicolino, Carlo Ratti
Structural Engineers: Domenico del Re
Coordinators: Carlo Ratti and Walter Nicolino

Alluvial Sponge Comb
Anderson Anderson Architecture
268-271

Solar Updraft Tower
Schlaich Bergermann Solar
272-275
272-273   Photo credit: bgp design, Stuttgart

Hawaii Gateway Energy Centre
Ferraro Choi and Associates
276-281   Photographer: ©2007, David Franzen
278   Credit: "Used by permission of
GreenSource; The Magazine of Sustainable
Design, a publication of McGraw-Hill Companies,
(page 71, Hawaii Gateway Energy Center)"

Tree
Simon Heijdens
294-295   2006-2007, location sensitive
outdoor projection.
Friedrichstrasse, Berlin (page 294)
Bank Street, New York (page 295)

Untitled (1.)
Ilkka Halso
296   2000, 'Restoration' series.
132.5 x 100 cm, edition 6.
68 x 52 cm, edition 10.

Museum I
Ilkka Halso
297   2003, 'Museum of Nature' series.
100 x 135 cm, edition 6.
50 x 65 cm, edition 10.

Dreamworld
Leo Fabrizio
298-299   2005-2007, 'Dreamworld' series:
POND (page 298), LAKE (page 299).
Bangkok, Thailand.

Pine Tree
Bae Bien-U
300-301   2005, C-print, 260 x 135 cm.
Courtesy of Gana Art Gallery

Vulkane
Nils-Udo
302-303   2002, Lanzarote, Canary Islands.
Fuji Flex on Aluminium
116.3 x 200 cm, edition 8

Roden Crater
James Turell
304-305   since 1979, © James Turell
Photographer: Florian Holzherr

Rainscape No. 49
David Fried
306-307   2005, Archival C-print, Plexiglas,
UV silicon, Alu-Dibond, Aluminium.
86 x 115 cm

Architecture of Change
Substainability and Humanity in the Built Environment

Edited by Kristin Feireiss and Lukas Feireiss

Design and layout by Birga Meyer for Gestalten
Art direction by Robert Klanten
Cover photo © Nic Lehoux
Production management by Martin Bretschneider for Gestalten
Project management by Julian Sorge for Gestalten
Proofreading by Patricia Mehnert

Printed by Eberl Graphische Betriebe, Immenstadt
Made in Germany

Published by Gestalten, Berlin 2008
ISBN 978-3-89955-211-9

Bibliographic information published by the Deutsche Nationalbibliothek.
The Deutsche Nationalbibliothek lists this publication in the Deutsche
Nationalbibliografie;
detailed bibliographic data is available on the internet at http://dnb.d-nb.de.
Respect copyright, encourage creativity!

For more information please check: www.die-gestalten.de

None of the content in this book was published in exchange for payment by
commercial parties; the editors selected all included work based solely on its
artistic merit.

This book was printed according to the internationally accepted FSC
standard for environmental protection, which specifies requirements for an
environmental management system.

Simon Heijdens
Tree

Ilkka Halso
Untitled (1.)

Ilkka Halso
Museum I

Bae Bien-U
Pine Tree

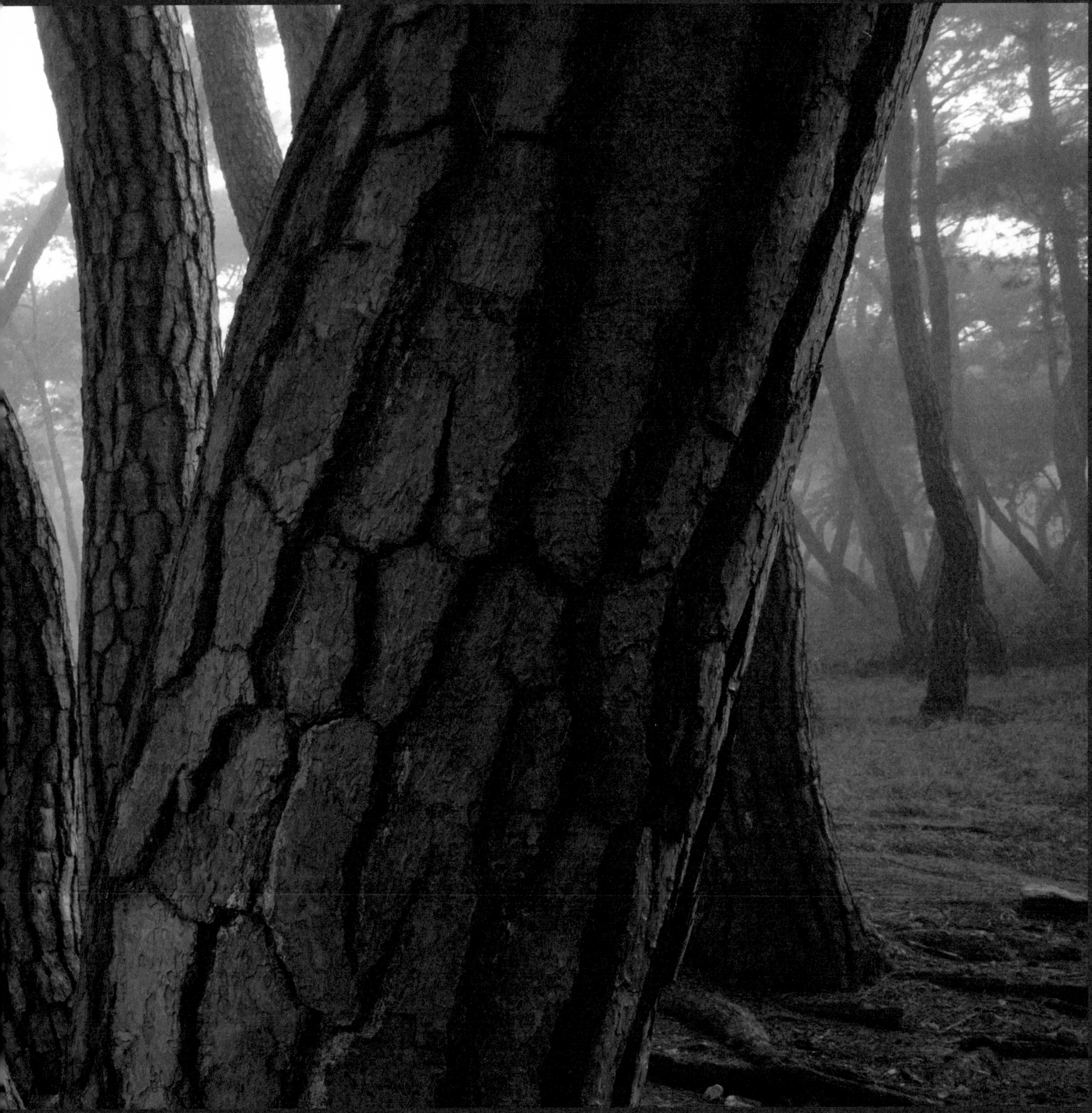

James Turell
Roden Crater

David Fried
Rainscape No. 49